LACE IN RETURN BOX to remove this checkout from your record.
O AVOID FINES return on or before date due.

DATE DUE	DATE DUE	DATE DUE
MAR 0 5 2003 4		

PRO-POOR AID CONDITIONALITY

POLICY

ESSAY

NO. 8

JOHN P. LEWIS

PRO-POOR AID CONDITIONALITY

POLICY ESSAY NO. 8

PRO-POOR AID CONDITIONALITY

JOHN P. LEWIS

OVERSEAS DEVELOPMENT COUNCIL

WASHINGTON, DC

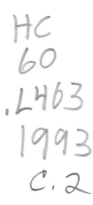

HC
60
.L463
1993
C.2

Library of Congress Cataloging-in-Publication Data

Lewis, John Prior.
  Pro-poor aid conditionality/John P. Lewis.

Policy Essay No. 8
Includes bibliographical references.
    1. Economic assistance—Developing countries. 2. Economic assistance, Domestic—Developing countries. 3. Poor—Developing countries. I. Title. II. Series.

HC60.L463   1993   338.9′1′091724—dc20   93-19137 CIP

ISBN: 1-56517-009-1

Printed in the United States of America.

Director of Publications: Christine E. Contee
Publications Editor: Jacqueline Edlund-Braun
Edited by Kallab Communications
Cover and book design by Tim Kenney Design Partners, Inc.

The views expressed in this volume are those of the author and do not necessarily represent those of the Overseas Development Council as an organization or of its individual officers or Board, Council, Program Advisory Committee, and staff members.

Contents

Foreword vii

Acknowledgments ix

Executive Summary 1

Introduction 6

The Record of Pro-Poor Development Policy 9

Menu of Conditionalities 12

Playing the Influence Game 17

Project Versus Nonproject Loans as Policy Instruments 17

Transfers and Reforms: Complements or Substitutes? 19

Recipient Pluralism 20

Deniability 20

The Number of Targeted Reforms 20

Donor Centralization or Decentralization 21

Coordination Among Donors 21

The Collision of Adjustment and Pro-Poor Programs 22

Pro-Poor Revisionism in the 1970s 22

The Content of the New Thinking 23

A Two-Pronged Basic Needs Agenda 24

The Poverty and Social Sectors Link 25

The Project Mode 25

Lessons That Emerged from the 1970s 25

Preemption: Conditioned Transfers for Adjustment 26

The Pro-Poor Challenge and a Partial Response **29**

Bringing Poverty Back In: A Fuller Response **31**

The Current State of Play: The World Bank **32**

The Bilateral Scene **36**

Pro-Poor Policy Instrumentation **41**

    Linkages **41**

        Enhanced Nonproject Adjustment Loans **42**

        Nonproject Nonadjustment Loans **43**

        Traditional Project (or "Investment") Loans **44**

        The "Neo"-Project Loan Option **44**

    Styles, Manners, and Modes **45**

Conclusions: A Changing Climate? **45**

Notes **49**

About the Author **51**

About the ODC **52**

Board of Directors **53**

Foreword

The collapse of communism and the end of the Cold War have led policymakers in both rich and poor countries to return to several longstanding issues of intrinsic importance: progress toward democracy, reducing military expenditures, protecting the environment, and focusing development strategies on poor people. Addressing these issues will not be easy and will require substantial policy change by all governments. The debate over how governments and international organizations can best promote reforms in other countries is growing in intensity. As a result, increasingly there are calls to put conditions on financial flows to and from poor countries to promote noneconomic policy reforms in the developing world.

The concept of conditionality is controversial in that it implies the use of leverage or coercion on the part of the wealthier—usually Northern and Western—nations to encourage shifts in policy and action within target countries—usually Southern and Eastern. Therefore, along with the scope and limits of conditionality, there is a need to assess the potential for alternative, more consensual approaches to the goals of the new international agenda.

Pro-Poor Aid Conditionality considers the extent to which the development community has and can in future apply conditionality for the goal of poverty reduction. This essay is the third in a series of systematic examinations of the scope and limits of conditionality issued by the Overseas Development Council. Other *Policy Essays* focus on the goals of supporting political reform, encouranging changes in the military sector, and the effects of multiple aid conditionalities. All of the essays start from the assumption that conditionality is only one of a broad range of alternative or complementary approaches to these goals.

The *Policy Essay* series provides a forum for authors to express opinions, make predictions, and assess policy ramifications in the field of U.S.-developing country relations. The relatively abbreviated format is a readable brief for policymaking, yet lengthy enough to allow room for more extended analysis.

The Overseas Development Council gratefully acknowledges The Ford Foundation and The Rockefeller Foundation for their support of the Council's overall program.

John W. Sewell
President
May 1993

Acknowledgments

The author gratefully acknowledges suggestions by Joan Nelson, Nicole Ball, John Sewell, Catherine Gwin, and Christine Contee, among others, and Val Kallab's usual fine editing. In particular, he would like to acknowledge the invaluable assistance of Stephanie Eglinton, especially with regard to the section on bilateral donors. All errors and omissions, however, are his own.

Executive Summary

Multilateral and bilateral donors of overseas development assistance are renewing their commitments to poverty reduction. While the plight of the poor in developing countries improved, on average, during the past three decades, the situation remains dire; the importance of pro-poor aid as a component of development assistance is undiminished. Both donors and recipients are learning how to make antipoverty aid transfers more effective and have recognized that recipients' policy contexts heavily determine project and other development outcomes. Thus, donors are bringing pressure to bear in behalf of recipient policy reforms—including those that strengthen the poor.

"Conditionality"—broadly defined as donor attempts to influence recipient behavior by means of resource transfers—can take various forms: the allocation of aid toward countries whose programs incline toward objectives the donor favors, covenants attached to projects, and nonproject or program lending that is policy-based. Nonproject assistance, epitomized by World Bank structural adjustment loans, has been favored recently as the most effective instrument for promoting policy change. The manner in which influence is conveyed can range from hard, didactic, before-the-fact conditioning to more interactive aid offered as a reward for good performance.

"Pro-poor conditionality" involves the confluence of three elements: pro-poor development policy, structural adjustment lending, and the instrument of policy conditionality. In the early 1980s structural adjustment lending by the World Bank began to displace antipoverty efforts directly targeting the poor that development assistance had emphasized in the 1970s. Policy conditionality, which was employed to achieve adjustment goals, became a rival to antipoverty efforts. The conflict became a matter of greater concern as the adjustment need proved to be less temporary than originally envisioned. Advocates of pro-poor development, notably UNICEF, argued that the policy adjustments promoted by the new lending were squeezing the poor in developing countries—often disproportionately.

As development strategies had to cohabit with ongoing adjustment, conditionality took on a kindlier look vis-à-vis the poor. First, adjustment efforts were amended with "compensatory programs" to cushion the burden on the poor. Second, while some donors began to question whether the tool of conditionality could not be used positively on behalf of pro-poor policy reform, the World Bank and others started including poverty reduction and social sector policies as sub-targets under "enhanced" adjustment programs. In *World Development Report 1990: Poverty*, the World Bank articulated a full reincorporation of poverty alleviation into basic adjustment strategy. The main branches of the Bank's antipoverty strategy were stated as efficient labor intensification and human-resource development, along with some targeted transfers and safety nets.

At the end of 1991, the World Bank issued a new Operational Directive on Poverty Reduction, committing both adjustment lending and investment (i.e., project) lending to an antipoverty focus. The directive required that all Bank operations be consistent with recipient antipoverty efforts. Indeed, the social sector content has been rising in World Bank adjustment lending. Yet, plagued with the pitfalls of target proliferation, the Bank may be shifting toward the use of other transfers to promote antipoverty reforms. It may find a greater role for stand-alone, nonadjustment, policy-based lending to achieve goals such as enhanced public employment or land reform. But, project loans may also be revamped to bring a policy-enhanced mix of advice and resources to bear on single pro-poor targets.

Bilateral donors' policies toward poverty and conditionality have been evolving in recent years, particularly as different governments have reevaluated their aid programs. Though many bilateral donors have been faithful defenders of the poor—channeling aid to the poorest people in the poorest countries—and have encouraged the World Bank toward greater antipoverty emphasis, they have not attempted much rigorous pro-poor conditionality of their own. Some have tended to view the imposition of stiff ex ante conditions on their transfers as invasions of recipient sovereignty. Lately, however, bilateral governments have increasingly engaged in policy-based lending, in most cases linking their undertakings to those of the World Bank and International Monetary Fund (IMF). The U.S. Agency for International Development has had extensive experience with policy-based lending of its own, for years having placed conditions on project and sector loans requiring such pro-poor goals as more attention to primary education and basic health. As conditionality is likely to have limited leverage for small amounts of aid, effectiveness requires bilateral donor coordination.

Multilateral and bilateral donors have several instrumental options when using aid operations to promote anti-poverty efforts by aid recipients. When determining their overall allocations of aid, donors can consider, along with other factors, how effectively recipients' policies strengthen the poor. Doing so, they engage in "allocative conditionality." The United States, Germany, and the Netherlands have recently developed systems of aid criteria geared along these lines, and, with its allocation of highly concessional funds through the International Development Association, the World Bank also engages in pro-poor allocative conditionality. Under the current operative formula for country allocations, performance, including poverty-alleviation performance, is the dominant consideration.

When conditioning a particular loan or grant, the World Bank and a few bilateral lenders have stretched the umbrella of adjustment lending to include pro-poor policy conditions, so that antipoverty goals have become integral subtargets of the loans. The option of "enhanced nonproject adjustment lending" has advantages such as mitigating the abrasive nature of adjustment and folding interventions that would been difficult on their own into omnibus loans. It also has heavy costs: the more policy targets and the more conditions any loan carries, the more problematic and weaker the enforcement of any individual condition tends to be.

The danger of target proliferation may be avoided by the use of a separate option: stand-alone nonproject grants or loans. In this case, a single instrument is matched with a single pro-poor or social-sector policy reform. World Bank SECALs focused on aspects of agriculture or education are examples of movement in this direction. Given the narrowness of the targets, however, conditions or covenants attached to project loans may serve the purpose just as well—provided that the policy purpose dominates the transaction and (preferably) that a transfer of persuasive size is available for local-cost funding.

Thus, traditional project-lending—in which the donor is mainly concerned with getting the project right—is no longer the only project-loan option. "Neo-project" lending and grant-making is emerging as an alternative in which the donor and recipient are engaged in dialogue regarding the need for pro-poor policy efforts. Both parties agree that the primary objective of the project or group of projects is policy reform in the sector of the transfer. While the difference between such policy-based project lending and nonproject lending may seem semantic, the former may avoid some of the political controversy associated with the latter.

Conditionality is a sensitive tool; recipient governments tend to resent intrusions on their policies. Generally, the manner and style of pro-poor conditionality is softening across the spectrum of multilateral and bilateral transfers. The tendency for more dialogue, more joint author-ship of policy goals, and more ex post conditioning leads to a more constructive and more congenial medium for leveraging pro-poor policy reform. Donors are more concerned that recipient governments "own" the reforms they make. When host governments participate not only in the implementation but also in the formulation of the policy agenda, the reforms both donors and recipients seek will be more likely to succeed.

It is heartening to see an enhanced donor emphasis not just on recipients' *need*, but on pro-poor performance. But if pro-poor conditioning is to be effective, donors must be prepared, from time to time, to turn off aid to regimes failing to make a credible effort to strengthen their poor.

Pro-Poor Aid
Conditionality

INTRODUCTION

■ THE END OF THE COLD WAR GIVES CITIZENS and governments of industrialized nations a chance to push overseas development policy harder in the direction of poverty reduction. Foreign policy priorities are up for review, and the case for stronger pro-poor efforts in what used to be called the Third World is powerful.

The heart of the case is a moral one: helping poor people, including whole countries of mainly poor people, to get on their feet is the right thing to do, and it is still needed. Over the past thirty years, the poor in developing countries have become better off on average, but their plight remains dire and improvable. Doing good is not, however, the only rationale for assisting the developing world's poor. With the changing international agenda has come a growing recognition of the linkages between the objectives of poverty alleviation programs and other desirable goals. Such programs can win markets for American and other developed-economy exports. They can be environmentally benign. They may slow down a global population bomb, and they may make the world safer and more politically stable. The World Bank had all of these considerations in view when its 1990 *World Development Report* declared "the fundamental issue in economic development" to be "the eradication of poverty from the world."[1]

The road to poverty alleviation often requires governments of developing countries to alter their policies. Donors and lenders can encourage reform through dialogue and persuasion. In the last few years, however, external development promotion agencies have increasingly called on "conditionality" as a tool to press recipient governments to more vigorous reform. Conditionality generally refers to linking the funding provided by an external government or agency to actions—in particular, policy reform—by a host government. The interesting poverty-conditionality issues arise in the context of official (multilateral and bilateral) transfers. The present discussion will confine its attention to such transfers, although without focusing exclusively on "aid." Thus we are interested in bilateral grants and loans as well as credits from the World Bank's International Development Association (IDA), which are concessional official development assistance (ODA). We also consider the kinds of nonconcessional official transfers provided by the International Monetary Fund (IMF) and by the World Bank out of the funds it borrows in financial markets.

Other *Policy Essays* in this Overseas Development Council series have explored the extent to which the development community can appropriately apply conditionality for the goals of political reform and reduced military expenditures. This essay will do the same for the goal of poverty alleviation. But the subject of conditionality is different in the antipoverty case because of the way that conditionality, pro-poor policy, and pro-adjustment policy all became doubly entangled during the 1980s. As to poverty alleviation, conditionality has had both a negative and a positive effect.

At the start of the 1980s, the development promotion community came to view poverty alleviation and policy conditionality as rival objectives. In a way, this was a curious confrontation, since the first of the pair was substantive and the second procedural. Poverty alleviation (combined with social-sector strengthening) was a *policy target;* conditionality was an *instrument* that could be used to advance a variety of policy goals. Logically, there could be no direct competition between the two.

What had happened was that policy "conditionality" became shorthand for the substantive goal of adjustment in whose behalf it was employed. "Adjustment" was itself an ambiguous concept. In the realm of macroeconomics, it long had referred to the kind of realignment of fiscal and monetary policies that the IMF favored for returning a country's aggregate demand and international payments to a sustainable, acceptably noninflationary path. But the second (1979–1980) oil shock—and the subsequent interest-rate shock it helped trigger—confronted many developing countries with a widening of their external payment deficits that did not look temporary or self-reversing.[2] The worsened trade deficit needed to be dealt with urgently (lacking some new lines of credit, countries could see themselves running into a commercial brick wall). "Dealing with it" required not just adjusting (i.e., "stabilizing") demand, but what the World Bank and others came to call "structural," supply-side adjustments of production patterns that would narrow countries' trade gaps and at the same time (in many cases) reduce their internal fiscal deficits.

So construed, the collision between adjustment and pro-poor (and social-sector) programs became clearer: it was partly budgetary. Programs to strengthen the poor and to raise human resources expenditures and investments typically required increased public outlays, whereas structural adjustment undertook to squeeze a different set of priorities into a constrained budget total. Because adjustment needs were not postponable in the early 1980s, major donors gave such programs the right of way and slowed their pro-poor, social-sector lending. This was the *negative* side of the story.

Although advocates of assistance to the poor and to the social sectors regretted this slowing from its very beginning, their initial complaints were tempered by assurances that adjustment's preemption of a larger share of official transfers was temporary. While the forces that had enlarged many countries' trade and budget deficits were thought to be enduring, the restructuring undertaken to close the deficits could be seen as a one-step exercise. Once the structure of production had been realigned over a medium term of a few years, the new balances should sustain themselves, and official transfers could revert to their old (including pro-poor) priorities.

As the 1980s proceeded, however, the image of adjustment as a temporary interruption in the antipoverty, social-sector agenda faded. Adjustment needs persisted. Indeed, in many countries they were compounded by an indigestible debt burden. It became clear that better ways needed to be found for the joint address of the poverty and adjustment agendas. But the questioning went beyond that: it began to be asked whether the instrument of conditionality could not also be used *positively*, in behalf of poverty reduction. This essay, then, explores the intertwining of three factors: pro-poor policy, structural adjustment policy, and aid and loan conditionality as an instrument deployable in each of these two substantive policy directions.

There are two other complications to the story. First, adjustment and poverty reduction did not remain clear-cut rivals. As operations evolved during the 1980s, some lenders/donors—notably the World Bank—broadened their definition of "adjustment" to encompass pro-poor policy reforms. (The relationships discussed in the essay are sometimes between a donor and a recipient and at other times between a lender and a borrower. For convenience I will hereafter use the term that most closely fits the context of the discussion.) Second, conditioned "policy-based lending" came to be identified with a particular type of transfer, namely, the nonproject loan or grant. How tight that fit actually needs to be will be considered later in this essay.

. . . .
THE RECORD OF PRO-POOR DEVELOPMENT POLICY

■   PARADOXICALLY, THE COLLAPSE OF COMMUNISM has permitted heightened attention to the poor at the same time that the interest of the American public and others in alleviating developing-world poverty has abated—for at least two kinds of reasons.

First, the swell of manifest destitution and homelessness in our own cities during the past decade or so has at once hardened us to the entreaties of the poor; signaled our collective inability to cope with poverty close at hand; and downgraded the claims of distant poverty. Second, confidence has been declining in the *effectiveness* of developed-country and multilateral attacks on developing-world poverty. The donor community, more particularly the United States, has been suffering a long-standing case of "aid fatigue." There is a sense that, for all the huffing and straining, pro-poor development assistance has accomplished little; that there are more poor people than ever in much of the developing world; that the gaps between rich and poor countries have widened; and indeed, that there are instances where aid has made matters worse.

Both of these enervating perceptions of antipoverty development assistance are misleading. In response to the first perception (without taking on the question of domestic antipoverty reform), one can assert confidently that the alleged trade-off between the domestic and developing-country agendas is illusory. *Within* the U.S. development assistance budget, there have indeed been trade-offs between pro-poor and so-called adjustment priorities. But development assistance claims such a meager slice of the U.S. federal budget, let alone of total gross domestic product, that resources can be found for enhanced domestic antipoverty programs (whether from a "peace dividend" yielded up by the defense budget or other sources) without encroaching on the development transfers sector. This point has just been made again and with care in ODC's alternative international affairs budget for FY1993.[3]

The other perception—the lack of confidence in aid's effectiveness—is wrongheaded both 1) about the reduction of poverty actually achieved in the developing world and 2) about the role of development assistance in that achievement. As to the first point, that many people in Asia, Africa, and Latin America remain poor after 40 years or so of pro-development effort should be the least surprising of findings. Poverty has been endemic nearly everywhere from the beginning of human history. What is remarkable is the extent of the inroads on poverty that have been made in the developing regions in the past few decades. From 1965 through 1989, for example, the annual growth rate of real gross national product (GNP) per capita averaged 2.9 percent in the world's developed market economies. The figure was measurably higher—3.1 percent—for the developing countries. Even more striking is that this was the *per capita* comparison while population was growing 2.3 percent annually in the developing countries and only 0.8 percent per year in the developed. Hence, compared with a figure of about 3.7 percent for the Western developed world, aggregate annual real GNP growth in these years averaged almost 5.5 percent for the developing world—probably higher than any comparably large group of countries had achieved during any previous quarter-century.

Moreover, these aggregate gains were not concentrated in the upper echelons of these internally very unequal developing societies. Table 1 shows that, during the periods covered, in all the countries included, although the absolute numbers of the poor rose in a few countries, the percentages of people who fell below national poverty lines declined. In addition, in nearly all cases the depth of poverty (i.e., the amount by which the average income of the poor fell short of national poverty lines) was also improved.

The United Nations Development Programme's *Human Development Report 1992* notes that, during 1960–1990, income disparities *among* the Southern countries have widened, as have the very-top to very-bottom income differences between North and South. But when one considers North and South as country groups, the human welfare gaps between the two have narrowed in a number of key dimensions: life expectancy,

TABLE 1. CHANGES IN SELECTED INDICATORS OF POVERTY

Country and Period	Length of Period (years)	Share of Population Below Poverty Line[a]		Number of Poor (millions)		Average Income Shortfall[a] (percent)	
		First Year	Last Year	First Year	Last Year	First Year	Last Year
Brazil (1960–80)[b,c]	20	50	21	36.1	25.4	46	41
Colombia (1971–88)[b]	17	41	25	8.9	7.5	41	38
Costa Rica (1971–86)[b]	15	45	24	0.8	0.6	40	44
India (1972–83)	11	54	43	311.4	315.0	31	28
Indonesia (1970–87)	17	58	17	67.9	30.0	37	17
Malaysia (1973–87)[b]	14	37	15	4.1	2.2	40	24
Morocco (1970–84)	14	43	34	6.6	7.4	46	36
Pakistan (1962–84)[b,c]	22	54	23	26.5	21.3	39	26
Singapore (1972–82)	10	31	10	0.7	0.2	37	33
Sri Lanka (1963–1982)[b]	19	37	27	3.9	4.1	35	29
Thailand (1962–86)[b,c]	24	59	26	16.7	13.6	—	35

Notes: This table uses country-specific definitions of the poverty line. Official or commonly used poverty lines have been used when available. In other cases, the poverty line has been set at 30 percent of mean income or expenditure. The range of poverty lines, expressed in terms of expenditure per household member and in purchasing power parity (PPP) dollars, is approximately $300–$700 a year in 1985—except for Costa Rica ($960), Malaysia ($1,420), and Singapore ($860). Unless otherwise indicated, the table is based on expenditure per household member.

[a]The average income shortfall is the mean distance of consumption or income of the poor below the poverty line, as a proportion of the poverty line.

[b]Measures for this entry use income rather than expenditure.

[c]Measures for this entry are by household rather than by household member.

Source: World Bank, World Bank Development Report 1990: Poverty (New York: Oxford University Press, 1990), p. 41.

under-five years mortality, daily caloric supply, adult literacy, and combined primary and secondary school enrollments.[4]

In short, the pro-development, pro-poor record in the developing world during the second half of the century nets out on the side of success. The record was considerably below average in Sub-Saharan Africa, and therefore above average in much of Asia and Latin America. But by historical standards, the overall performance, for all its incompleteness, has been surprisingly good.

As to the second issue—whether external development assistance shares any of the responsibility for this achievement—it would be odd if it did not, for such aid has been unique to this era of improved growth and equity in the developing world. Assistance has had many forms, guises, and degrees of effectiveness. Certainly some of it has been wasteful, not oriented toward development or poverty reduction, and/or conducive to dependency. Moreover, foreign aid is bound to be procedurally awkward. It has to interact at arm's length with regimes of widely different qualities and capacities, all of which, however, are keenly mindful of their sovereign autonomy. Yet aid has had major successes—for example, its contributions to South Asia's "green revolutions" of the 1960s and 1970s and to East and Southeast Asia's economic restructuring in the 1970s and 1980s. Absent aid, the erosion of welfare in much of Sub-Saharan Africa during the past 15 years would have been much worse. Serious studies of aid effectiveness repeatedly have answered, "yes—on balance," to the question posed by the title of one of them, *Does Aid Work?*[5] Further, the same studies, reviews, and evaluations have taken note of some lesson-learning; aid agencies, while their memories sometimes are short, have tended to correct earlier miscues.

If one is concerned with helping the disadvantaged in poor countries, official development assistance represents a body of experience and practice worth building on while also reforming. The improved knowledge about what works together with the opportunities of the post-Cold War era argue for redoubling efforts to combat poverty. This makes the impact of aid "conditionality" on poverty alleviation an important current issue.

· ·

MENU OF CONDITIONALITIES

■ THE MULTIPLE AVAILABLE DEFINITIONS of conditionality and some of the procedural issues implicit in them need to be considered before one sets out the essay's main argument. The thrust of the term "conditionality" as it is used in transfer operations is clear enough: it involves an attempt by the donor, in the course of making the transfer, to influence recipient behavior—either activity directly related to the subject of the transfer, or something else. As Figure 1 suggests, one can construct a whole menu of more and less inclusive conditionality concepts.

The matrix takes account of three kinds of variance:

1) How broad are the issues in question? Do they encompass the whole array of national priorities, or particular (macro and/or sectoral) policies, or single, discrete projects?

2) Through what procedures is influence wielded? These can range from soft to hard as indicated by the two vertical cells of the matrix.

3) There is a second procedural issue (separate because it is not necessarily correlated with the other modalities): How weak or strong is the donor's enforcement of an agreed undertaking?

The matrix identifies three kinds of "conditionality," broadly defined, that arise in the case of pro-poor assistance (and indeed they relate to other policy targets as well, but here the focus will be confined to poverty). The first type, sometimes called *allocative conditionality*, is based on a donor's overall assessment of the question: Does the recipient's general seriousness and effectiveness as a promoter of the poor motivate donors, as partisans of the poor, to allocate more or less aid to the recipient than they would if they had a neutral perception of the recipient's antipoverty stance? Bilateral donors, in particular, have recently emphasized this approach. In terms of procedural style, there is no way allocative conditionality can be other than soft. To attempt to be a hard, didactic conditioner, a donor would have to try to take over the recipient's whole governmental function; this would be impossibly intrusive. Yet, against a background of dialogue, a donor may well be very hard-nosed in *enforcing* its assessment of a recipient's general priorities. If the donor agency does not like what it sees, it can reduce aid or stop it entirely.

One example of allocative conditionality in behalf of the general pro-poor orientation of a country's development effort might be the support that certain bilateral donors—notably the Dutch and the Nordics (and also the World Bank during Robert McNamara's presidency)—gave Tanzania in the 1970s. These donors consistently gave a disproportionate

FIGURE 1. A MENU OF CONDITIONALITIES

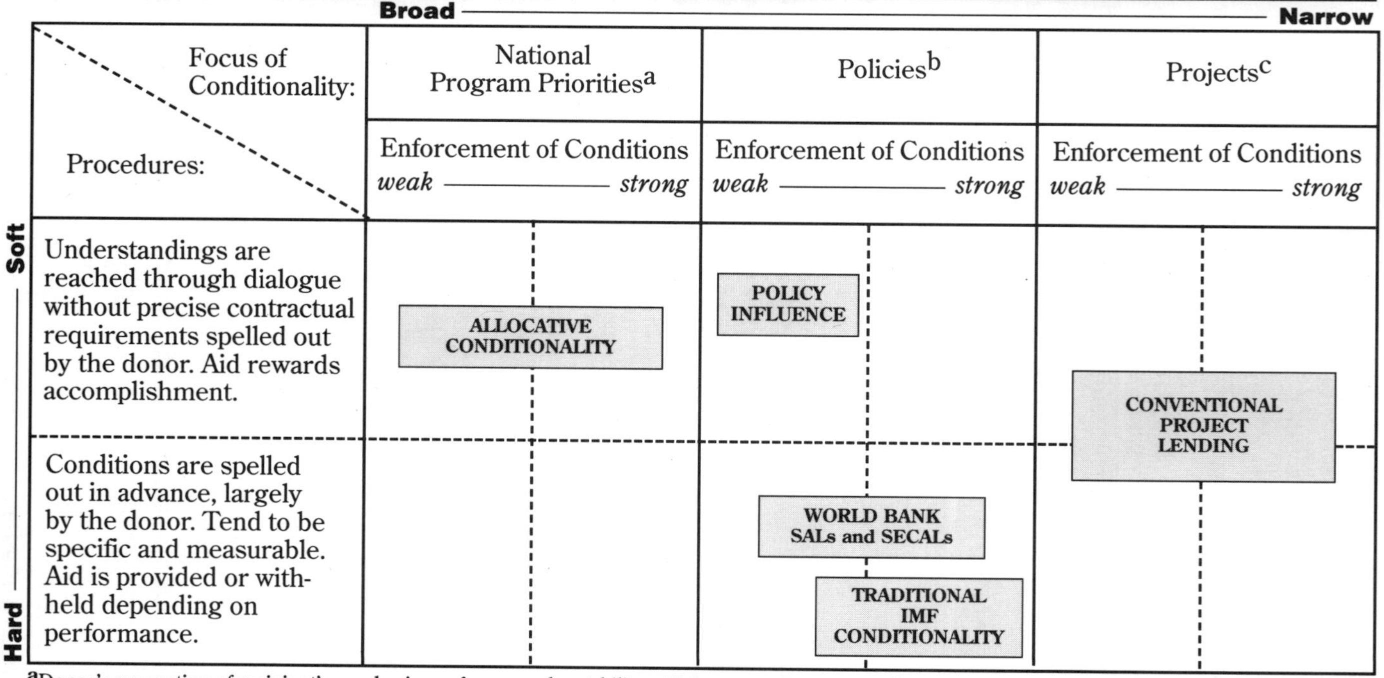

Broad ————————————————— Narrow

Focus of Conditionality:	National Program Priorities[a]		Policies[b]		Projects[c]	
	Enforcement of Conditions		Enforcement of Conditions		Enforcement of Conditions	
Procedures:	*weak* ——— *strong*		*weak* ——— *strong*		*weak* ——— *strong*	
Soft — Understandings are reached through dialogue without precise contractual requirements spelled out by the donor. Aid rewards accomplishment.	ALLOCATIVE CONDITIONALITY		POLICY INFLUENCE			CONVENTIONAL PROJECT LENDING
Hard — Conditions are spelled out in advance, largely by the donor. Tend to be specific and measurable. Aid is provided or withheld depending on performance.				WORLD BANK SALs and SECALs / TRADITIONAL IMF CONDITIONALITY		

[a] Donor's perception of recipient's emphasis on, for example, stability; efficient growth, poverty alleviation, environmental protection, or nonbelligerence, as compared with other recipients under consideration. [b] Policy decisions—either macro, sectoral, or subsectoral—for example, a change in exchange rates or agricultural price policy, or cutting subsidies for grain crops. [c] Discrete bounded investments either physical or institutional, for example, an irrigation project or the reform of a particular irrigation agency.

fraction of their scarce ODA resources to Tanzania in recognition of what they saw as the Nyerere government's exceptional commitment to improving the situation of the poor.

The most conventional form of conditionality, involved in *conventional project lending,* is shown at the right side of the matrix. In the "covenants" of the project loan, the conditions are explicit; they are written by the donor, and their implementation is monitored and rigorously enforced. But, as the overlap of this form of aid with other cells of the matrix suggests, the preceding is a stereotype. Often the borrower has a great deal of input into the design as well as the implementation of the project. And in the cases of many donors, many of the project covenants are only weakly enforced.

As a modality, project conditionality is familiar and relatively noncontroversial. It is hard to think of a project loan that does not stipulate technical specifications to which the borrower agrees and actions and resources it undertakes to contribute to the joint endeavor. This is true when the objective is to build a dam. But it is just as true when the substantive thrust of the project is directly pro-poor—say, when it diverts aid to education from higher education to primary education, which more directly and broadly benefits the poor.

It is mostly in the *recipient's policies* column of the matrix, however, that the interesting and conflicted elements of the "poverty conditionality" story lie. Policies, in contrast to projects, are things about which host governments are sensitive and where donors' intrusions are inherently abrasive. This is true even when it is evident that the donor's dominant purpose is the development of the recipient; the implication still is that the donor has better answers than the recipient to pervasive problems that lie within the recipient's sovereign domain.

Because of this sensitivity, the manner in which—indeed, the manners with which—policy influence is conveyed can be all-important. As the matrix indicates, the modalities of conditionality can vary from soft to hard. Hard is not necessarily more effective. But it is crisper, tougher, and appears less ambiguous. It is the style of conditionality typified by standard IMF standby operations:

1) The borrower wants some additional IMF credit.

2) The Fund lays down a precise set of macroeconomic reform moves and targets (in the areas, for example, of exchange-rate

and domestic budgetary management) that, before it gets the loan, the borrower must pledge to make and/or reach.

3) Then, with this *ex ante* mode of conditioning, whether the borrower gets a second tranche of this loan or a second, follow-on loan is advertised as depending on the rating the borrower's performance of the conditions gets when the lender evaluates the performance—although, as the matrix indicates, in practice, the lender's *enforcement* of conditions can vary from strong to weak.

The IMF's enforcement of conventional standbys has tended to be strong: the conditions are quantified and unambiguous, and the Fund has the reputation of requiring borrowers to toe the line. Procedurally, the World Bank's structural adjustment loans (SALs) were created in the image of IMF standbys. Yet enforcement—partly for reasons of greater complexity and less precision in the conditions but partly also for other reasons to which we will come—has tended to be less strict than the Fund's.

At the soft (upper) end of the matrix's policy column are various forms of "dialogue." Here the conditionality (broadly defined) is less didactic, more interactive—and *ex post*. The donor plants (and receives) ideas. The recipient fine-tunes the policy designs. When the recipient enacts a reform that has evolved from the interaction between the parties, the donor responds with a celebratory loan or grant.

Recently the World Bank had some difficulty explaining such a case to its Board of Executive Directors. Management proposed a SAL to Indonesia without tranches. The directors demanded to know: How did management propose to enforce the policy conditions? The answer was that the Indonesian government, with which the Bank characteristically has had quite constructive and amiable relations, had, after discussion with the Bank, already taken the reform steps that the SAL stipulated it should take. Sometimes soft and hard modes of policy conditioning can work in tandem. In the mid-1960s, the author and others in the U.S. Agency for International Development (USAID) mission to India were involved in a great deal of interactive dialogue with the government of India, especially its agricultural ministry, about agricultural reform. USAID nonproject loans were triggered by India's adoption of reforms that the dialogue apparently had helped bring about. But at the same time, President Lyndon Johnson was "short-tethering" food aid to India to provide *ex ante* leverage in behalf of the same reforms.

. . . .

PLAYING THE INFLUENCE GAME

■   NOW THAT THE MENU OF CONDITIONALITY concepts has been laid out, there is no need to exclude any of them from the present discussion. The focus of the essay, however, remains on *policy* conditioning—for and against poverty alleviation. There are a few other points about playing the policy influence game that need to be made before turning to the recent (mixed) history of the "poverty-conditionality" relationship in the following sections.

PROJECT VERSUS NONPROJECT LOANS AS POLICY INSTRUMENTS

Throughout the post-World II era of official lending and grant-making to developing countries, most donors have preferred the project mode of transfer. Some, such as the World Bank, have been mandated by their constitutions to be project specialists, but even when they have not been so constrained, most donors (like virtually all commercial banks) have shared the preference for funding discrete units of development activity (whether in the form of capital or technical assistance projects)—without, as it were, taking on the whole national system in which the project is lodged.

Some of the rationale for the bias in favor of projects was illusory: it was not, in fact, possible to insulate project performance from the national policy environment. With national governments retaining their prerogatives over currency convertibility, one could not be sure that a project with a good internal rate of return would repay the foreign lender. Nor was it socially optimal to exclude projects (e.g., in education) whose benefits did not accrue to the project unit. Moreover, thanks to the fungibility of resources, it was not easy to impose sectoral or subsectoral priorities on a reluctant borrower.

Nevertheless, the project mode of transfer has afforded the donor an unparalleled opportunity to help shape the character of the project itself—its conception, its design, its appraisal, its counterpart funding by the recipient, and its implementation. The opportunity often has been partially wasted, but there is little doubt that it exists.

What has become a lively question as donors have become less inhibited about trying to influence recipient policies, however, is whether project loans can do double duty as conveyors of ideas. Can they serve both to get the project "right," or more nearly right from the donor's perspective, and *also* to bring influence to bear on broader policies of the recipient? Over the years, donor agencies (and, indeed, factions within donor agencies) have been of two minds about this issue. Advocates of continued reliance on the project mode of development funding have argued that a donor can use a set of projects, a "program of (several) projects," to transmit its broader policy advice to a recipient government. They have argued that the concept of project is itself elastic and can be stretched to proportions to which broad policy conditions can quite appropriately be attached. Moreover, donor funding of local project costs has been advanced as a quasi-substitute for nonproject lending: by allowing the recipient to make flexible use of the foreign exchange provided, project loan funding of local costs matches one of the advantages government borrowers find in nonproject loans. This may (the project people have argued) make the borrowers more attentive to the messages that such loans convey not only about project details, but also about broader policy issues.

By 1980, however, the preponderance of opinion in donor agencies had jelled on the side of the nonproject (or "program") loan as the better vehicle for policy advice. For example, in 1982, the World Bank's Operations Evaluation Department, in its Eighth Annual Review of Project Performance Audit Reports, stated that "[on] the basis of experience it would be reasonable to conclude that individual projects in general are inefficient instruments for inducing policy change."[6] The theory of this conclusion was that it was indeed usually difficult to kill two birds with one stone—to get the project right *and* to get the recipient to attend as well to another policy issue. The patience of the recipient was likely to have been exhausted by the project transaction per se. Second, it was awkward—almost implausible—to try to make a narrow instrument (a discrete project loan) bring pressure to bear on a broad policy target. Greater symmetry worked better.

By now the experience of various donors tends to corroborate such theorizing. Several bilateral donors, notably USAID, have grown fairly accustomed to the practice of policy-based *program* lending. Such, of course, is the only kind of lending that the IMF does in the short-to-medium time frame within which that institution works. What sealed the current dominance of the nonproject vehicle as a carrier of policy influence, however, was the World Bank's launching of its SALs in 1980—supplemented, shortly thereafter, by Sectoral Adjustment Loans (SECALs). With this shift, and despite its mandated project emphasis, the Bank made the nonproject loan (always before a marginal aspect of its operations) the central instrument of its policy reform thrust—and therefore the presumptive (although not necessarily exclusive) vehicle for all subsequent policy conditioning.

TRANSFERS AND REFORMS: COMPLEMENTS OR SUBSTITUTES?

Policy-based lending involves the use of a loan or a grant to promote change in recipient policies. The transfer and the reform are seen as complements. The donor buys itself a place at the policy table—either creating an *incentive* for the borrower to adopt the recommended reform, or, by cushioning some of the reform's by-product effects (say, a squeeze on urban consumers, or the burst of imports unleashed by trade liberalization), making adoption *feasible*.

There is, however, the contrary possibility: transfer and reform can operate as *substitutes*. The transfer can become a crutch that permits the recipient government to lessen its own effort or postpone an adequate course of reform. How these countervailing effects of reform-targeting transfers interact depends upon the country, the policy in question, and recent history. But a conventional view is that complementarity dominates in early phases of policy-based lending. Recipient reform mounts in response to the external input. But then if the latter becomes large enough, substitution takes over, and indigenous effort tops out. For the policy-based lender, the trick is to feed reform without enervating it.

RECIPIENT PLURALISM

The fact that most recipient regimes are not monoliths (the same can be said of donor regimes and such multilateral intermediaries as the World Bank) is what makes policy-based lending as feasible a venture as it is. When a recipient government is four-square against a proposed reform, there is no way an external lender can force acceptance of the reform or, at least, its survival in the medium term. Outsiders have a chance of promoting reform only when there are sympathetic factions within the government whose hands the donor can strengthen.

DENIABILITY

The issue here goes to the strong versus the weak subcolumns in the earlier matrix. It is often said that the credibility of the *ex ante* policy conditioning process depends on the demonstrated willingness of the donor to turn off the transfers when it becomes dissatisfied with the recipient's performance of the conditions. This is broadly true, although the threat of withdrawal sometimes has served as a close substitute for the real thing. What is precisely true, however, is that if a transfer is to serve well as a pro-reform lever, the borrower must not doubt the lender's political and psychological capacity to deny it. It is for this reason that food aid often is a less effective policy lever than a general-purpose non-project loan. If the food is urgently needed, it may seem implausible to the recipient that the donor would let children starve to make its policy point.

THE NUMBER OF TARGETED REFORMS

The IMF's traditional conditioning has focused on a limited range of policies and therefore has addressed a predictable and limited number of targets. The World Bank, by contrast, has adorned most of its SALs and SECALs with a remarkable array of policy conditions—an average of as many as 56 per loan in recent years, according to one of the Bank's self-assessments.[7] While the Bank seems to be the worst practitioner of this Christmas-tree effect, many donors are still learning the lesson that to diffuse the focus of policy-based lending is to dilute its effectiveness. This concern, indeed, is part of the rationale for the present Overseas Development Council series of Policy Essays. As the conditionality process is stretched to cover new subjects, presumably employing the same loan/aid vehicles, how much does the proliferation of targets weaken the instrument?

DONOR CENTRALIZATION OR DECENTRALIZATION

How the policy influence game is played depends to some extent, in the case of donors, on where their key players are located—overwhelmingly at agency headquarters or also in the capitals of recipient countries? An agency such as USAID, which is comparatively decentralized geographically, has had resident missions with enough size, seniority, and delegated authority to sustain most of the Agency's interaction with the host government. This organizational model is more conducive to modes of influence at the dialogue, interactive end of the procedural spectrum—compared with such a highly headquarters-centered operation as the World Bank, which depends more on itinerant missions for its operational interchanges with borrowing governments. At the same time, the transient mission may be a more effective, if less amiable, device for pressing the recipient to decide a difficult issue.

COORDINATION AMONG DONORS

Finally, the extent to which the dozens of donors and lenders—bilateral, multilateral, official, nongovernmental—that provide transfers to most developing countries are coordinated in their support of selected policy objectives clearly can have major effects on how the policy influence game is played. Lack of coordination can mean that the presence of other, less demanding suppliers can undercut the pressure that a reform-minded donor seeks to bring to bear on the recipient. Conversely, donor coordination, typically centered around a lead donor such as the World Bank and often articulated via a formal consortium or consultative group, can multiply the leverage that the lead donor can impart to its policy program (although, since the other participating donors are not sheep, coordination may modify, if not dilute, the program).

From the recipient side, donor coordination usually looks like "ganging up." On the other hand, it is accepted as a means of augmenting the total volume of transfers received. And, as noted, there may be factions within the regime that agree with the intended reforms and therefore welcome donor coordination as a means of enhancing reform prospects. Even more generally, if the alternative is to be hit simultaneously, from different quarters, by several hard policy conditions that are not only uncoordinated but conflicting, most recipients would prefer to have the donors get their acts together.

· ·
THE COLLISION OF ADJUSTMENT AND PRO-POOR PROGRAMS

■ THE SURGE OF CONDITIONED STRUCTURAL adjustment lending at the beginning of the 1980s collided with the stream of pro-poor, social-sector uplift efforts that had been building through the 1970s.

PRO-POOR REVISIONISM IN THE 1970s

The whole international effort to promote growth and development in Asia, Africa, and Latin America could be conceived as an assault on developing-world poverty—and some saw it that way. But by the end of the 1960s, awareness was spreading that generalized development promotion—pejoratively dubbed "trickle down"—was not a good enough means of addressing the plight of the poor and disadvantaged in developing countries. Not only had the on-average strong developing-world growth of the 1960s widened the disparities *among* developing countries, but also *within* many countries, the poorer and weaker segments of the population had shared very little in the national gains. Most of the revisionist critics had no desire to abandon growth promotion. But they wanted it supplemented by various more *direct* attacks on poverty and disadvantage.

As the 1960s turned into the 1970s, such policy views began to crop up all over. Reformist thoughts were voiced in the annual reports of the U.N. Committee for Development Planning. There was a trace of them in the 1969 report of the World Bank-sponsored Pearson Commission on development and aid, and a much stronger strain in the 1970 commentary on the Pearson report organized by Barbara Ward and featuring such activists as Mahbub ul-Haq.[8] The U.S. Agency for International Development began to invest in research on income distribution in 1972, and in 1973, the United States was pushed by the Congress into a "New Directions" strategy for development assistance that concentrated on poverty alleviation and key dimensions of social welfare. Similar focuses characterized other bilateral donors as the decade proceeded. The International Labour Office (ILO), previously preoccupied with developed-country labor relations, found a new mission for itself in a World Employment Programme launched in the early 1970s, featuring a set of revisionist assessments of the pro-poor development needs of several particular developing countries (Colombia, Kenya, Sri Lanka, and the Philippines).

Quickly, however, the dominant voice in the revisionist camp became that of Robert McNamara, who assumed the presidency of the World Bank in 1968 with an agenda emphasizing poverty alleviation and began calling for rapidly accelerating World Bank investments in pro-poor projects especially by IDA. After some forerunning comments in earlier statements and documents, McNamara in September 1973 gave an address to the joint Bank/Fund annual meeting in Nairobi, Kenya, that became (along with the ILO's document for its landmark global conference on basic needs in June 1976) one of the seminal texts of 1970s' revisionism.

THE CONTENT OF THE NEW THINKING

The fact that the overt subject of the McNamara's Nairobi speech was rural development—more particularly, small-holder agriculture—nicely illustrates how sectorally multifaceted, yet conceptually integrated, the decade's revisionism was. Thanks partly to the ILO initiative, one of the earlier emphases was on the poor's need to be rescued from underemployment. But their need was not just for more work; it was for more income. And while there was interest in redistribution (like USAID, the Bank-sponsored studies of income distribution), there was greater concern with attacking "absolute" poverty at the low end of the income array. There was a focus perforce, albeit not exclusively, on rural poverty, because countrysides were still the regions in which most of the developing countries' poor people lived. And because small-holder farmers in many countries were the largest groups accessible to policy (absent land reform, it often was harder to reach the landless), agricultural uplift for small-scale farming tended to be the program of choice. At the same time, for reasons to be indicated, the revisionists preferred to address rural development in the round—with agriculture at the core but with attention also to related infrastructure as well as human-resource and institutional development.

Something like a consensus along these lines began to emerge among aid providers and many developing-country regimes in the 1970s. Three of its central elements warrant particular emphasis.

A TWO-PRONGED BASIC NEEDS AGENDA. When basic needs" (or later, "basic human needs") became another honored objective in the revisionist vocabulary on the occasion of ILO's 1976 conference, the concept had an unexpected tilt. In common sense parlance, basic needs invoked certain minimal standards of welfare—along with nutrition, such public goods as basic health and educational services—as essential components of an acceptable standard of living. Unmet basic needs invite transfers of resources, from richer to poorer people domestically or from donors abroad, to lift the needy up to the minimum standards.

But this was not the main "basic needs message" in 1976. The ILO agreed with the Bank, other donors, and many developing-country governments: the only feasible way to raise the real incomes of the poor masses was to raise their productivity—hence, the two-pronged approach. Resource transfers were still needed to provide safety nets under the old, young, and incapacitated, but transfers could not begin to handle the main job. That must be tackled by programs to help the weak and disadvantaged build their productive capacities.

THE POVERTY AND SOCIAL SECTORS LINK. This point overlaps with the preceding one. Poverty alleviation and social-sector strengthening (or, alternatively, human resource development) are paired throughout the essay, and the rationale for this linkage became clear in the 1970s. It was not just that the poor's standard of living was exceptionally dependent on such public goods as health and educational services. If the poor were to earn most of their real-income gains in a self-help mode, they needed more assets. Yet most of the poor were in rural areas, and in most countries it was politically difficult to break loose more land for the rural poor. Policy, therefore, needed to build their *human capital*. It needed to make them healthier, more literate, better trained, better able to space their children. It needed to pursue these goals by means of various social-sector programs and the kinds of institution-building that these required.

THE PROJECT MODE. Nearly all donors in the 1970s conveyed the antipoverty and substantively related aspects of their assistance in a project format. As noted, this was their preferred and, in several important instances, their mandated mode. In some cases, notably the World Bank's, there was a struggle to maintain rigorous standards of appraisal and implementation while pushing steadily increasing sums through the project channel. But there was little thought of abandoning the format. In the case of rural development, in particular, this had an important consequence. Rural development "in the round" involved not only the agricultural production function together with inputs and marketing; it was seen to extend to credit institutions and cooperatives as well as training, education, health, population, and other social services. The project format motivated aid designers to build all these facets into single complex, hard-to-synchronize schemes—and then, since recipient governments seldom had the ready-made administrative capacity to implement such *tours de force*, to hire the best managers and technical personnel away from the regular bureaucracy into special project authorities— thereby weakening the regular bureaucracy.

LESSONS THAT EMERGED FROM THE 1970s

By the end of the 1970s, when development cooperation was overtaken by the adjustment crisis, direct attacks on poverty were still only gaining stride in parts of the aid arena. Nevertheless a good deal of experience had accrued, and the decade's revisionist thinking had itself undergone a number of revisions[9]:

■ Participation was much more in vogue. Earlier poverty alleviation had undertaken, from the top-down, to do good things for the poor. The need for bottom-up efforts (often involving external and/or indigenous nongovernmental organizations) to help the poor become more self-reliant was more widely credited.

■ Complex, multifaceted rural development projects were commonly seen not to work. There was renewed hope that, as Albert Hirschman had argued, one-thing-at-a-time advances would create pulls on associated sectors and activities.[10]

■ Pouring all inputs into discrete, site-specific projects diverted both donors' and recipients' attention from building national institutions and national cadres of professional and paraprofessional expertise.

■ Special project authorities fell under the kind of cloud already suggested.

■ It became increasingly apparent that external, especially official, interveners in behalf of the poor were better wholesalers than retailers of resources. They needed to create challenges and incentives to indigenous authorities to become better retailers.

■ Experience revealed some substantive flaws in the pro-poor work of the 1970s. For example, much of what had been done under the rubric of agricultural credit was open to challenge.

■ Many felt that donors, notably the World Bank, had pushed money into pro-poor projects in the 1970s faster than was consistent with the maintenance of good quality control.

But all such lessons simply pointed to the need for some course corrections. There is no reason to think the 1970s thrust of pro-poor assistance would not have been sustained had the adjustment priority not intervened.

PREEMPTION: CONDITIONED TRANSFERS FOR ADJUSTMENT

The second oil shock (1979–1980), leading to and compounded by the ensuing interest-rate shock, under circumstances where commercial-bank lending to developing countries was beginning to dry up, confronted many developing countries with an urgent need for fast-disbursing official transfers. They required more resources for longer terms than they could get from the IMF, since the widened payments deficits they were obliged to cover (due to higher oil prices and escalated interest rates) were going to require time-consuming adjustments in the countries' production and trade structures. Developing-country governments were in the market for fast-disbursing (presumably nonproject) loans, whether concessional or nonconcessional, from bilateral donors and the multilateral development banks.

The World Bank, in particular, was prepared to respond, but it also saw the situation as an opportunity. During the 1970s, the Bank had been becoming more and more mindful of how critical borrowing countries' national policy environments were in determining development outcomes. At the same time, the Bank had been building more (and it thought *better*) in-house policy-analysis capacity. But the institution had been frustrated by the mismatch between this capacity and the vehicles available, namely, project loans, for conveying its policy advice to borrowers. As policy instruments, project loans suffered the infirmities indicated earlier in this essay; yet the Bank's program lending had been marginal and exceptional.

Thus the World Bank seized on the new demand for official quick-disbursing, medium-term money as an opportunity to convert program lending into one of its central activities (albeit one still accounting for only a minor fraction of its portfolio) *and* to impose on the new vehicle a heavy load of broad (macro and sectoral) policy conditioning.

Although at first viewed skeptically by some of the Bank's executive directors, the new structural adjustment lending program took off rapidly. From early 1980 to mid-1986, 38 SALs were made to 20 countries, and by the end of that period another 25 were in the works. To qualify, countries needed both 1) to have suffered an unbalancing and presumptively enduring set of (mainly external) shocks and 2) to display the political will to undertake corrective reforms. The 1980 *World Development Report* already put the number of eligible borrowers in the vicinity of 80; and Bank management, in a 1981 report to the board, stated that "[t]he Bank has been willing to consider requests for a SAL in *all* cases in which a government has presented a program which adequately addresses the country's adjustment problems, or which provides the basis for formulating such a program, and where the government has been willing to reach agreement with the Bank on a monitorable program of action."[11]

The early SALs were more hand-tailored than the typical IMF stabilization program. Yet they had a set of strong common themes. In its first review of SAL experience (1986), the Bank's Operations Evaluation Department enumerated three:

1) Increasing exports on the basis of comparative advantage to ease the foreign exchange constraint and [revive] economic activity.

2) Greater use of market forces and more realistic pricing in domestic and foreign trade . . . to improve the efficiency of resource use and enhance . . . competitiveness . . . .

3) Better management of public sector operations . . . to raise . . . returns on public spending and reduce . . . deficits.[12]

The new SALs were medium-sized. It was not clear that the new loans were made in lieu of *non*adjustment (i.e., project) lending to the SAL-receiving countries themselves; on the contrary, in several cases *both* kinds of lending increased. But in the aggregate, there was some diversion. Certainly this was true of IDA, where total resources were clearly bounded, as was mainly the case with bilateral donors of ODA. While the latter did not instantly follow the Bank's initiative, by 1986–87 at least a half-dozen members of the OECD's Development Assistance Committee (DAC) were doing program lending explicitly targeted on policy reform.[13]

By the mid-1980s, Bank-IDA program lending (now overwhelmingly SAL and SECAL), which had been about 10 percent of the institution's total lending before the SAL initiative, had more than doubled. This meant that, quantitatively, while there had been some displacement of project lending, adjustment loans and credits were still far short of dominating the Bank's portfolio. Nevertheless, those who identified with development assistance's previous antipoverty push saw two reasons for concern.

First, although it claimed only a minority share of Bank-IDA money, the new adjustment lending claimed a majority share of top management's time, attention, and nervous energy. As a priority, poverty alleviation had been downgraded.

Second, the policy adjustments promoted by the new lending appeared to be squeezing the developing world's poor—either disproportionately or at least, given their vulnerable condition, painfully. It was this issue that generated countervailing efforts from within the ranks of development-assistance agencies.

....

THE PRO-POOR CHALLENGE AND
A PARTIAL RESPONSE

■   UNICEF IN THE EARLY 1980S WAS the first to pose the issue of whether the developing countries' poorer and weaker classes did not need some cushioning against the impacts of the policy adjustments other international agencies were promoting and funding.[14] Initially, UNICEF pursued the question particularly with the IMF, focusing on that agency's demand-adjustment or stabilization programs.[15] But quickly the questioning spread to World Bank SALs and SECALs, and, indeed, to pro-adjustment lending on the part of bilateral donors.

The adjustment funders were concerned that adjustment promotion not be blamed for injuries to the poor that were the fault of countries' underlying economic mismanagement, which adjustment reforms were trying to put right.[16] There was also debate about whether adjustment policies squeezed the poor more or less than their better-off countrymen. Here, in retrospect, we can say it depended on which policies were enacted (which tax increases, which expenditures cuts, etc.) and who the poor were (rural small-holders, landless laborers, urban poor, etc.)[17] At the same time it was (and remains) clear that effective reforms to narrow a country's external-payments and domestic-budget gaps almost invariably put a country through a period of austerity. Moreover, even if the reduction in activity is distributionally neutral, the poor are the more exposed. They have fewer reserves; they tend to suffer more; and they need anti-adjustment cushioning on humanitarian grounds.[18]

These arguments played well in the mid-1980s. Many in the multilateral adjustment lending agencies themselves had been thinking along the same lines, and so had bilateral donors. In due course, after program amendments had been worked out with recipients and multidonor efforts had been coordinated, various country- and region-specific responses to the warnings about adjustment's impacts on the poor began to appear. Two were conspicuous. In Bolivia, the government itself took the lead in 1986 to organize the Social Emergency Fund, a temporary support program to follow up a radical fiscal and monetary adjustment. Established outside regular government channels, the Social Emergency Fund undertook to raise and disburse quickly (for a broad array of infrastructure and social and entrepreneurial assistance projects) large quantities of additional external resources. In Ghana, the Programme of Action to Mitigate the Social Costs of Adjustment (PAMSCAD) was launched in 1987. Although initiated by the Ghanaian government, PAMSCAD had elaborate international participation. No less than eight multilateral and bilateral agencies, chaired by the World Bank, contributed to the design, and more signed on for implementation.

These "compensatory" initiatives were, to various degrees, replicated in other countries and fed into the Social Dimensions of Adjustment project established by the World Bank and the United Nations Development Programme (UNDP) in Africa. Implementation of the compensatory efforts has been disappointing, however. The Bolivian do-it-yourself case was loose-jointed, although it delivered a quantity of resources quickly. PAMSCAD in Ghana was, in its design and procedural requirements, extremely complex. The compensatory "safety net" projects—notably in PAMSCAD—cushioned the income and employment impacts on civil servants better than on anyone else and only lightly reached the poorest, especially in rural areas.[19]

Beyond these particular shortcomings, the UNICEF leadership found the Bank's response partial—and wanting. As of 1987, they saw the Bank still treating the needs of the poor as inviting merely a compensatory supplement to basic structural adjustment programs, whose basic character should not be disturbed.[20] This was not an isolated criticism. It was implicit in the pronouncement that DAC donors as a group had made in their high-level meeting at the end of 1986:

> . . . [The members of the DAC] agree that structural
> adjustment programmes should take fully into account

equity and income distribution issues and would like to
see more explicit addressing of budget and strategy issues
in human resources questions such as education, health
and population.[21]

But if the Bank's defense of the poor was too narrow, the leading
adjustment lender was about to broaden its response. And as will be
indicated more explicitly later in this essay, junctions between aid conditionality and pro-poor policies were evolving for several bilateral donors
as well.

. . . .

BRINGING POVERTY BACK IN:
A FULLER RESPONSE

■ THE UNICEF LEADERS HAD A RIGHT to feel they had been
misunderstood. The adjustment funders heard them asking for compensatory, antipoverty add-ons to adjustment loans—whereas, virtually from
the beginning, compensation was only one of a considerable set of revisions
that UNICEF's James P. Grant, Richard Jolly, and their colleagues were
proposing be made in adjustment loan design.[22] Indeed, already in the
1984 paper to the IMF, and certainly in its trademark work on the subject
Adjustment With a Human Face, UNICEF was calling for a reshaping
of adjustment policy from the ground up.[23]

It could be argued that, even in its original formulation by the
World Bank in the early 1980s, adjustment theory had not been explicitly
sequential; it had not been, first adjustment, then growth, and then—
only later and perhaps—get back to poverty alleviation. The original
justification for adjustment was to protect and enhance growth—compared to what otherwise would have transpired.[24] The same theme, adjustment *with* growth, was accented in the so-called Baker Plan for debt
accommodation of October 1985. But now the UNICEF team wanted
poverty alleviation not as an afterthought but, like growth promotion,
built in as a basic and integral part of adjustment policy.

In the World Bank there was growing receptivity to this idea
during Barber Conable's presidency (1986–1991). Partly to signal the

return of the subject toward center stage, it was decided to do another *World Development Report* on poverty (together with the social sectors, poverty had been the subject of the 1980 *WDR*). When it appeared, *World Development Report 1990: Poverty* articulated a full reincorporation of poverty alleviation into basic development (and adjustment) strategy. The report saw sound antipoverty policy as consisting mainly of "two equally important elements." The first was to promote choices of efficient, labor-intensive products and modes of production in order to raise the employment, productivity, and income of the poor. The second element was to build the productive capacities of the poor by providing enhanced basic social services such as primary health care, family planning, and primary education.

These two main branches of the Bank's pro-poor policy were seen, after allowances for timing and budgeting, to be reconcilable with both growth and adjustment strategies. The first—efficient labor intensification—was fully congruent with growth promotion. It also was conceptually compatible with efficiency-seeking adjustment. Adjustment, however, also has an austerity aspect that, in curbing demand, is apt to produce temporary unemployment. Thus, although labor-intensive restructuring will translate a given amount of demand into more jobs, for a while total demand may fall short of the employment need.

Similarly, the second main branch of Bank antipoverty strategy, human resources development, certainly is in harmony with growth promotion. But its budgetary needs are likely to be at odds with adjustment's austerity requirements, necessitating either offsetting reductions in other public outlays or revenue increases if adjustment and poverty alleviation are to be reconciled.

. . . .

THE CURRENT STATE OF PLAY: THE WORLD BANK

■ THE WORLD BANK HAS BEEN A practitioner of pro-poor "allocative conditionality" (although it has not known the phenomenon by that name) at least since the launching of the International Development

Association at the start of the 1960s. The unbroken practice of IDA is to allocate all its credits to the poorer developing countries, i.e., those whose gross national products per capita fall below a specified (and over time gradually rising) ceiling. Like all pro-poor transfers, however, IDA allocations encounter a dilemma: Should the distribution be weighted toward need or self-help? Toward the level of poverty or level of antipoverty effort?

As noted above, via the mechanism of the ceiling, the country poverty level factor is built into all IDA country allocations. *Within* the set of IDA countries, however, a recent revision of the allocative formula has given increased weight to countries' poverty alleviation *performance.* It should be made clear that country-size and high-policy parameters framing the whole IDA distribution greatly distort the per capita allocations. Thus, it is agreed that China and India, although they account for two-thirds of the IDA-eligible population, should share no more than 30 percent of the distribution. Similarly, although the Sub-Saharan African countries represent a far smaller fraction of the population, they get no less than 45 percent of total credits; and countries with populations below two million get disproportionately large per capita shares.

Nevertheless, the IDA distribution is more consistently population- and poverty-responsive than that of most other donors. Under the currently operative formula for normative or putative country allocations, "performance," including poverty alleviation performance, is the dominant consideration. Performance consists equally of short-run economic management (mainly of demand), longer-run economic management (mainly restructuring), and poverty alleviation effort. Each of the three reflects composites of the rating assigned by knowledgeable Bank staffers to subdimensions of each policy category. Thus, in the poverty alleviation case, the policies evaluated include the delivery of social services as well as reforms removing distortions from labor markets and rural-urban terms of trade.

According to the Bank's 1989 reckoning, whereas a "moderate" overall performance rating gives typical countries in the 2–50 million population range an annual normative allocation of SDR 5.36 per capita, a "low" performance is good for only SDR 2.72, and a "high" performance creates an entitlement to SDR 8.75. At least as impressive is the variance induced by differing performances in the poverty alleviation category alone (with the economic performance in all three cases being held to the midpoint of the range): moderate poverty alleviation, SDR 5.36; low, SDR 4.49; high, SDR 6.30.[25]

Finally, one cannot claim, of course, that these entitlements, as we have just called them, are precisely translated into annual country-by-country aggregates of IDA loans received, but over short, multi-year periods, they provide substantial guidance to actual operations.

We turn to the Bank's use of conditioned loans to promote particular pro-poor *policies* (the middle column of the matrix on page 14)—whether singly or in company with a variety of other policy targets (as in the enhanced adjustment loan case).

The Bank has been taking credit for a rising incidence of social-sector content in its adjustment lending. Thus, according to a recent in-house review, whereas only 7 percent of 60 adjustment loans incorporated social-sector conditionalities during 1979–1985, and only 11 percent of 85 loans during 1986–1988, the proportion rose to 33 percent of 60 loans during 1989–1990.[26] Moreover, these appear to have been social-sector operations that were tilted toward disadvantaged groups. For example, Chile, Gabon, Guinea, and Togo were pressed to redirect social-sector expenditures to the poor via primary education and primary health care programs; and Ghana, Indonesia, Kenya, Malawi, Niger, Senegal, and Sierra Leone were all encouraged, while raising social-sector user charges, to exempt the poor.

The case that the Bank's renewed pro-poor focus is more than cosmetic is easy to make. Both of the two latest presidents seem to have been strongly wedded to it, and the recent procedural implementation has been impressive. The very end of 1991 saw the issuance of a new Operational Directive on Poverty Reduction and an amplifying "hand-book." The lineage of the two traced back to *WDR 1990*. They provide that "every Bank-supported operation should be consistent with the [recipient country's] poverty reduction strategy." Subject to administrative and fiscal feasibility, "all adjustment operations should provide for safety net protection for the most vulnerable." In addition, where country circumstances warrant, adjustment operations should "address distortions that especially disadvantage the poor and support a reorientation of public expenditures towards infrastructure and social services for the poor." The directive and the handbook detail a regime of country economic and sector analysis to support an intensified focus on poverty. Included are public expenditure reviews and country poverty profiles and assessments. As noted, the directive explicitly provides that henceforth the "volume of lending should be linked to country efforts to reduce poverty."

What is equally striking about the new operational documentation, however, is that, having committed adjustment lending to an antipoverty focus, it is equally strong in enlistment of "investment" (i.e., project) operations. The latter are to be "designed to raise the productivity of the poor's physical assets, develop their human capital, improve their living standards, and/or provide a safety net." Moreover, the adjustment cum investment antipoverty agenda that the directive contemplates does not mention a place for nonadjustment, nonproject, policy conditioned loans.

This last may be sufficient ground for seeing the poverty reduction directive as another indication of some bending back by the Bank toward greater reliance on project lending.[27] But, if so, the kind of investment or project loan involved would not be quite the traditional project loan represented in the far right-hand column of the matrix. What may be in prospect are project loans conceived mainly as vehicles for single-policy messages consistent with the span and content of the loan. In April 1992, the Bank wrote a loan to Morocco that was still called a SAL. But this one provided in part that the government pursue a set of year-by-year incremental goals with respect to its allocations to primary education, primary health services, and the provision of health personnel to women in childbirth. The government was also enjoined to maintain a specified array of indicators by which education and health welfare could be monitored.

One can imagine the Morocco loan being quite easily converted into either one or a pair of project loans—if one assumption can be granted. In case the educational and health activities to be supported did not require enough commodity and equipment imports to use up a loan of the size judged to be policy-persuasive, the balance would need to be provided as local-cost funding. Lending for local costs presses on the boundaries of the operating modes projected for the World Bank in its Articles of Agreement much as nonproject lending does, but the former probably is politically less controversial. A shift toward such single-subject project loans may be the direction in which more of the Bank's future pro-poor, policy-based lending moves.

. . . .

THE BILATERAL SCENE

■ BILATERAL DONOR APPROACHES TO POVERTY and conditionality are also evolving as governments reevaluate the objectives of their aid programs in the context of challenges and opportunities in the post-Cold War setting. Differences in perspective among donor governments on both poverty alleviation and the use of conditionality as an instrument are reflected in the varying pace and direction of bilateral policies. In addition to persuasion through direct policy leverage and dialogue, bilateral donors can use other aid-related approaches to influence recipient policies that affect the poor. They can urge the World Bank and other multilateral institutions to press more aggressively for pro-poor policies, and they can take recipient government efforts in behalf of the poor into account in determining their inter-country allocations of aid. The following briefly reviews some of the approaches that different bilaterals have taken recently.

Since the conception of their aid programs, the *Nordic countries* have considered poverty alleviation their guiding principle and have deliberately channeled a high percentage of ODA to the poorest groups in the least developed countries. When the World Bank was revising the formula for aid allocation to IDA countries, the Nordic countries pressed the Bank to give pro-poor elements greater weight in the performance criteria. They have also become increasingly engaged in public expenditure reviews, jointly with the World Bank, where they stress the importance of spending on social sectors. Regarding the appropriateness of using conditionality to push for reform, however, these donors have been the prototypical skeptics—but they recently have come to agree that aid-receiving governments have to accept responsibility for the maintenance of effective policies. The Nordic countries prefer the "softer" style of persuasion through interaction and dialogue, but they have been taking advantage of their close ties with aid recipients such as Mozambique to push for policy reform, albeit without stated timetables.

In 1991, the *Netherlands* produced a remarkably comprehensive policy document reflecting its decision to shift attention and resources from economic investment back to poverty reduction. The policy was reinforced by the implementation of an extraordinary set of "development screening" instructions: every activity must pass the "poverty test" by persuasively showing that it will have at least some positive effect on poverty alleviation, women, or the environment.[28] There is no way any functionary could assemble and cross-weigh the great variety of data specified and otherwise work her or his way through the country analysis prescribed without becoming deadly serious about the recipient pro-poor needs. At the same time, the Dutch are reluctant to play a strident conditionality game. They address pro-poor policy concerns during routine consultations with recipient governments. Moreover, the Dutch are engaging in budget support programs that offer free foreign exchange to countries that are willing to improve their policy toward the social sectors but are fiscally constrained.

In 1988, *Canada* adopted a new aid policy framework in which poverty alleviation remains the top priority. Canada also continues to urge the World Bank and the Inter-American Development Bank to include more programming directed to the poor. Opposition to putting conditions on aid has dissipated since Canada began structural adjustment lending in the late 1980s, although most policy conditioning is linked to Bank and Fund lending. The Canadian International Development Agency (CIDA) pushes for pro-poor policy reform through dialogue with recipients on two levels: general macroeconomic policy and attention to social sectors. CIDA also uses the interesting tactic of bringing pro-poor pressure to bear on recalcitrant recipient governments by channeling more of Canada's subsequent assistance through nongovernmental organizations.

Germany's Federal Ministry for Economic Cooperation (BMZ) announced in 1991 a new system for determining country aid allocations that includes a checklist of political, economic, and social indicators to be considered in the case of each aid recipient. One criterion is the recipient government's commitment to development, including the measures being taken to assist the poorest populations. The Ministry intends this new procedure significantly to redirect aid allocations.[29] The BMZ's operational guidelines also provide that projects that "fight poverty through self-help" must benefit the poorest 50 percent of the population and involve the recipient government in design and implementation.

The *United Kingdom's* aid program and country allocations are strongly oriented toward poverty alleviation. As the country's aid budget has been constrained by other claims on public outlays (a problem for most bilateral donors), the Overseas Development Administration has managed to keep a high percentage of its allocations targeted on the poorest groups in poorer countries. The United Kingdom has become increasingly concerned about "good governance" and has stated that is prepared to cut aid when certain policy conditions are not met. Like others, while it is supportive of the World Bank's lead in the area of policy-based assistance and is encouraging the Bank toward a greater antipoverty emphasis, it is not attempting much pro-poor conditionality trail-breaking of its own.

Aid from *Japan* traditionally has been growth-focused and has paid less specific attention to poverty. In recent years, however, Japan has been implementing major changes in its program. Partly in response to international pressure, the percentage of grants in Japanese official development assistance—while still lowest among DAC donors—is increasing. The Ministry of Foreign Affairs reports that in 1990 about two-thirds of both its capital grant aid and its technical cooperation was addressed to meeting basic human needs.[30] In a special "Official Development Assistance Charter" issued in June 1992, Japan laid out the principles that it intends to consider when allocating aid in the future. Along with the country's established commitment to human resource development, the Charter focuses on poverty relief as well as human rights, democracy, environmental conservation, and reduced military expenditures. To the degree the new Charter is implemented, Japanese aid can be expected to change dramatically.

A strong defender of the principles of sovereignty and nonintervention, Japan chose to avoid getting drawn into the procedural stresses and intrusions of policy conditioning. It has preferred project aid, in which the borrowing countries identify and request the projects, over program aid. In 1987, however, Japan began a program of nonproject grant assistance—$500 million during FY1987–FY1989 and $600 million during FY1990–FY1992, primarily to needy African countries—for structural adjustment support. Nevertheless, instead of becoming another separate and additional policy advocate and conditioner, Japan is using its aid to reinforce and facilitate policy conditioning by others, mainly the World Bank.

The foreign assistance program of the *United States* is skewed toward advanced developing countries like Israel and Turkey and, compared to other donors, channels a low percentage of its aid to Africa. This tilt is expressed in the priority the United States has accorded the geopolitically motivated Economic Support Fund (ESF). U.S. development assistance (i.e., the main part of the U.S. program other than ESF), however, tends to be focused on agriculture, health, and education sectors, which are "closest" to the poor and require the greatest public investments in the poorer countries.

U.S. pro-poor strategy is similar to the World Bank's in that USAID uses a broad definition of poverty alleviation that extends beyond the social sectors. Poverty alleviation explicitly *is* the goal of structural adjustment, and USAID has the same "two-part-plus" program that the Bank has proposed: more labor-intensive employment and more human resources development, supplemented by some safety net and public employment add-ons. USAID urges attention to the poorest of the poor and to environmental needs, but in general it parallels the Bank's inclusive adjustment-cum-antipoverty agenda.

In keeping with USAID's tradition of decentralization, the different regional bureaus have been detailing their own systems of allocation criteria. Thus the Bureau for Latin America and the Caribbean uses the following weights: 50 percent to the country's adjustment policy, 20 percent to the quality of government (i.e., degree of democracy), 20 percent to the level of its social indicators, and 10 percent to the adequacy of its environmental policies. Attending to trends rather than social indicators, the Bureau for Africa considers the equity and efficiency of policies in such fields as agriculture, education, health, and population. Like other donors, USAID tries to allocate aid in a way that will maximize the impact of its antipoverty transfers, but in the antipoverty field as in others, its allocations are distorted by Congressional earmarking and (as noted) by foreign policy considerations other than development.

While most bilateral, policy-based lending is linked to the World Bank or the IMF, USAID has had long experience of its own with such lending. For many years it has placed conditions on sector loans, requiring such things as more attention to primary education compared with universities and to basic health compared with hospitals. USAID may also employ clusters of projects designed to achieve a policy objective collectively. Currently, social and/or agricultural subsector project loans in negotiation or in place (for example, in Guatemala, Ecuador, Jamaica, Brazil, Senegal, Mali, and Niger) are conditioned—without any particular fanfare about being policy-based—upon a related policy reform by the recipients. In Malawi, for example, USAID has an agriculture sector loan in place that has prompted the government, in the interest of small farmers, to cease confining burley tobacco production to large estates. Within a year, smallholders had raised their income by growing a superior crop that sold at premium prices; and tobacco estate laborers had obtained higher wages due to the diminished supply of estate labor.

As to procedures, bilateral donors gravitate toward the softer, dialogue end of the procedural spectrum. The power of persuasion is probably the most effective tool an individual donor has to influence recipients' antipoverty policies. Yet harder variants of conditionality can be useful instruments; the latter's effectiveness depends on the country circumstances surrounding both borrower and lender, as well as the relationship between the two. As small amounts of aid are likely to have limited leverage, effectiveness depends on donor coordination. As indicated, calls for renewed antipoverty emphasis have appeared at the collective DAC level as well as in the deliberations of particular country consortia and consultative groups. Particularly when the required policy conditions are complex and long term, donors need both to coordinate with one another and to support the reform process with technical and financial assistance.

As for the choice between project or nonproject loans as vehicles for policy conditions, donors, such as the United States, experienced with the nonproject instrument probably will continue to use it (although, compared to the Bank, they have much weaker adjustment-umbrella rationales for the choice). But the bilaterals are at least as familiar as the multilaterals with the project mode, and there seems to be no reason why single-subject policy conditioning to benefit the poor cannot, just as in the Bank's case, be conducted in this format—perhaps, in the case of the bilaterals also, letting the "conditioning" lose some of its sharper edges.

. . . .

PRO-POOR POLICY INSTRUMENTATION

■ THE CENTRAL THEME OF THIS ESSAY is procedural. Conditionality is here construed broadly as donor efforts of one kind or another to influence recipient policies. In the case of *pro-poor conditionality*, the relationship between means and ends started off negatively: conditionality as a means for promoting adjustment appeared to shoulder aside some of the pro-poor priorities and policies of the 1970s. More recently, the poverty-related conditionality question has been whether the tools of conditionality can be brought to bear positively, in behalf of poverty reduction. But, as we also have seen, an intermediate question has emerged, particularly in the case of the World Bank: Should poverty reduction and social-sector policies be included as subtargets under an enhanced (and conditioned) adjustment program?

The experience reviewed poses two kinds of instrumentation issues: 1) choices of the *linkages* to be made between recipient activities and types of donor-transfer vehicles; and 2) choices of the *styles, manners, and/or modes* of loan conditioning.

LINKAGES

Multilateral and bilateral donors confront the same alternatives. If they hinge the amounts of their total transfers to a country at least partly on how effectively the recipient's whole policy program strengthens the poor, they are (under the nomenclature used in this essay) engaging in "allocative conditionality." Both the Bank and a number of the bilaterals do some of this. It is a comparatively nonconfrontational procedure, since, almost by definition, it cannot convey precise donor-to-recipient policy instructions; even the most overbearing donor cannot pretend to prescribe the details of a whole national policy design to one of its sovereign clients.

Thus allocative conditionality is a blunt instrument. Yet it is not necessarily soft; it can be wielded suddenly and emphatically by a disenchanted donor.

This analysis suggests that donors who, instead of (or in addition to) giving their whole inter-countries allocation a pro-poor tilt, wish to link *particular* loan or grant operations to particular recipients' policies toward their poor have four instrumental options: enhanced nonproject adjustment loans, nonproject nonadjustment loans, traditional project loans, or, in order to differentiate them, what I am calling "neo"-project loans.

ENHANCED NONPROJECT ADJUSTMENT LOANS. In the World Bank and some of the bilaterals, pro-poor goals have become integral subtargets of adjustment loans. In and around the Bank, in particular, a set of forces has been favoring the enlargement of the adjustment/loan target set. The other subjects of this ODC series of essays—more democratic governance and constrained defense spending—as well as such other goals as environmental protection—have been urged upon the Bank by their advocates as additional SAL conditions. Within the institution, bureaucratic dynamics favor target proliferation: Different specialists are keen to gain leverage for the activities in which they specialize, and for the managers in charge of adjustment-loan vehicles, the easiest course is to let the new passengers aboard.

External considerations lean in the same direction: adjustment is an abrasive business; it helps to give it a human face and a green hat. Moreover, the Bank's board might block some stand-alone interventions, e.g., in behalf of reduced defense spending or improved governance, or ask how separate nonproject loans can be written in support of such objectives; it is easier to fold them into an omnibus adjustment loan.

Finally, there has been a fiscal accountability argument for including pro-poor targets under the adjustment umbrella. Core adjustment reforms are likely to call for austerity. Many pro-poor reforms demand public expenditures. Covering both reforms in the same loan underscores the need for a self-conscious reconciliation of their competing financial pulls.

These pro-poor inclusionary considerations attach with varying degrees of cogency to some of the SECALs into which the World Bank and a few other official lenders have divided their adjustment operations since the early 1980s. The advantages of stretching the adjustment umbrella in such cases are much the same as they are with SALs.

But (for both SALs and SECALs) such adjustment stretching also poses severe costs. There is a risk of ambiguity. Is the pro-poor element in the enhanced adjustment loan serious, or only lip service? Is not introducing the mantra of poverty alleviation into everything the donor does rather like declaring victory? More unmistakably, target proliferation imposes another cost. The more policy targets—and the more conditions—that any given loan carries, the weaker the enforcement of any one condition tends to be. The donor either pulls back from lowering the boom over the infraction of a single condition—or *does* lower it, creating a sense of injustice (i.e., disproportion between penalty and infraction) that diminishes the donor's ability to influence future policy.

It may be partly for these reasons that the World Bank, at present, seems to be taking pains not to put all its antipoverty eggs into the enhanced adjustment basket. Along with other donors, it has three other linkage options.

NONPROJECT NONADJUSTMENT LOANS. This is the option to which many expected the renewal of the 1970s pro-poor thrust to lead once the first surge of adjustment lending was past: If conditioned nonproject loans were the better vehicles for policy influence, why not let them also be put to the service of stand-alone, pro-poor and social-sector policies? As discussed earlier, in the World Bank in the late 1980s this possibility was upstaged by the extension of the adjustment umbrella to pro-poor causes. But the nonadjustment, nonproject option remains. In the Bank, SECALs—focused, for example, on education or aspects of agriculture—already are a step in this direction; and, compared with comprehensive adjustment loans, they represent a partial escape from the target proliferation pitfall. In the years ahead, both bilateral and multilateral lenders may find a use for stand-alone, conditioned nonproject loans in support of such policy changes as enhanced public employment or land reform.

At the same time, this loan category may well turn out to be a nearly empty set. The rationale for turning to nonproject instead of project loans in the first place was to get an instrument broad enough to match the breadth of a set of macropolicy targets. As important as they are, most pro-poor and pro-social-sector reforms are comparatively narrow targets conceptually—no wider than those of many traditional project loans. What is wanted from the recipient government, along with administrative and regulatory changes, is the commitment of domestic resources. These are precisely the kinds of commitments that can be covered in the conditions and covenants of project loans.

TRADITIONAL PROJECT (OR "INVESTMENT") LOANS. The possibility that conditioned lending in behalf of poverty alleviation may be reverting to greater reliance on the project loan vehicle does not, however, bring our story full circle. Conventional project loans, wherein the donor is predominantly preoccupied with getting the project "right," will continue to have the problems they always have had as carriers of *policy* influence—even conceptually narrow, single-sector policy. Traditionally, the donor's priority is to contribute to the creation of a discrete increment of (hard or soft) productive capacity rather than to reform policies shaping the field in which the project is being built. Thus, although the appearance may be the same, the "neo"-project lending to which linkage choices may be shifting is something rather different.

THE "NEO"-PROJECT LOAN OPTION. Investment lending is beginning to occur in which both parties acknowledge the primacy of policy reform. As with traditional project loans, the commodities the loan buys are inputs to a particular, usually site-specific, project; and certainly the parties are not indifferent to the quality of the project *qua* project. But there has been on-going dialogue about needed changes in pro-poor policies, and in this context both parties see the single-subject loan as being principally intended to promote the reforms upon which the loan is conditioned. To this end, the loan typically will supply a persuasive amount of foreign exchange in trade for the local costs it undertakes to fund. The term *neo-project loan* for the new investment lending alternative is arbitrary and may imply too sharp a differentiation, but I believe the distinction exists.

While the difference between such policy-based project lending and the nonproject lending it may displace comes close to being semantic, it is not trivial. Even if a neo-project loan's stipulations and conditions are just as onerous as those of a SAL or a SECAL, they may be less politically abrasive. In the minds of recipient bureaucracies, parliaments, and publics, abrasive conditionality has come to be tightly associated with nonproject lending.

STYLES, MANNERS, AND MODES

In terms of manners and process, the preferred mode of pro-poor conditionality is becoming more interactive across the whole spectrum of official multilateral and bilateral lending and/or grant-making. There is a shift toward more dialogue, more joint authorship of reforms, more flexibility in the definition of policy goals, and more *ex post* as against *ex ante* "conditioning." This tendency, which is evident in the multilateral development banks as well as the bilaterals, has a mixture of motives. In part it is defensive: particularly in the case of multitargeted policy loans, reactive *ex post* conditioning is less subject to being exposed as toothless.

But softer interactive conditioning, along with being favored by recipients, also is perceived by such donors as the World Bank to have strong positive virtues. One concern is what the Bank has taken to calling the "ownership" of reforms. No reform agenda, pro-poor or otherwise, can amount to much for very long if the recipient government—the host government—does not adopt it as its own. And such adoption, such "ownership," is more likely to occur if the host government participates heavily in the formulation as well as in the implementation of the agenda.

The other great advantage of a participatory reform process is closely related. The policy changes emerging from joint recipient-donor policy analysis are not only likely to be more successful because the recipient has a heavier stake in them; they are also likely to be intrinsically superior thanks to the input of the recipient's knowledge and experience. Two heads often continue to be better than one.

. . . .

CONCLUSIONS: A CHANGING CLIMATE?

■ IN ADDITION TO THE SPECIFIC INSTRUMENTATION possibilities summed up in the preceding section, a number of broader lessons emerge from this examination of the poverty-adjustment-conditionality interface.

In this period of redirection and recommitment, both the multilateral and bilateral institutions that promote development are (and should be) giving renewed emphasis to aiding the poor in poor countries, especially in ways that strengthen their capacities to help themselves. Although pro-poor development assistance is difficult to design and implement, much of it has worked reasonably well; both donors and recipients have been learning how to make it more effective; and if political will is not lacking, there is abundant scope for increasing the modest claims that pro-poor aid makes on our resources.

Both aid recipients and aid donors have become aware that recipients' policies—including their pro-poor policies—tend to dominate development project outcomes. Although developing-country governments are jealous of their policy autonomy, most of them now do recognize the right of multilateral and bilateral aid agencies to encourage recipients to effect constructive reforms. (Indeed, from the perspective of donor taxpayers, this is more than a right; it is the duty of aid agencies.)

Hoping that their aid will facilitate needed reforms more than substitute for them, donors undertake, in some form or other, to condition their transfers on recipient policy changes. But some kinds of loans and/ or grants serve better than others to convey such influence. The dynamics of traditional project lending are best adapted to getting particular projects "right." In the experience of many donors, broader (nonproject or program) loans are better suited to the promotion of policies whose impacts extend well beyond the reach of single projects. Such has been the thesis of the World Bank's structural adjustment lending begun at the beginning of the 1980s.

For a time in the 1980s, pro-poor aid was upstaged, if not preempted, by adjustment assistance. But then came efforts, first to render the latter fail-safe with respect to the poor, and thereafter, especially at the World Bank, to make poverty alleviation an integral and prominent component of what this essay calls enhanced adjustment lending.

In this latter role, pro-poor policy renewal has tended to rebalance the Bank's and other donors' development strategies. But it has also both aggravated and been victimized by policy-based, nonproject lending's worse pitfall—target proliferation. Donors, with the World Bank well out in front, have festooned their adjustment loans with more and more policy conditions—thereby weakening the enforceability of any one of them.

Belatedly, a rule of parsimony may be spreading in the corridors of policy lending design. We may see greater effort to match single loan instruments with single policy targets (or only a few) and to reserve the broadest (nonproject) instruments for the broadest (macro adjustment) targets. Under such a regime, pro-poor policy lending and the social-sector lending associated with it can be expected to stand more on their own instead of being folded into omnibus adjustment loans.

Which form this stand-alone, pro-poor, policy conditioned lending will take is uncertain, and it may vary by donors. Some of the latter may find scope for conditioned, single-subject, nonadjustment, nonproject loans. But there could instead be a shift (the World Bank may be veering in this direction) toward a new kind of investment lending, in which what are here called "neo"-project loans, growing out of a context of ongoing donor/recipient policy dialogue, will be primarily (not secondarily) aimed at promoting reform in the sector or subsector in which the loan's investment is lodged.

The turn toward "neo"-project lending, if it comes, will be frankly tactical: policy conditioning has been fixed in the public mind in developing countries as an abrasive business, and it is tightly associated with nonproject loans. Project conditioning, on the other hand, is a routine process. Even new-style, it may have a lower silhouette than adjustment lending. Moreover, if neo-project lending were commonly to be directed into local-cost funding, even its foreign-exchange attractiveness for recipient governments could come to rival that of nonproject loans.

The procedures—the manners—of pro-poor conditioning also may be moving in the direction of less stress. The IMF standby was an unfortunate model for development lenders. Interactive dialogue and *ex post* conditioning offer a more constructive as well as a more congenial medium for the leverage of pro-poor reform. The emphasis on recipient "ownership" of reforms is the healthiest preoccupation to have overtaken the aid business in some time.

Somewhat like having spoken prose all these years, all donors engage in "allocative conditioning" of one kind or another, and it is heartening to see an enhanced emphasis not just on poverty need, but on pro-poor *performance*. If the cause of pro-poor conditioning is to remain robust, however, then donors must, without attempting to micro-manage recipient policies, let the blunt instrument fall from time to time. Now and then they must simply turn off aid to regimes failing to make a credible effort to strengthen their impoverished classes.

Notes

[1] *World Development Report 1990: Poverty* (New York: Oxford University Press, 1990), p.7.

[2] When the oil shock revived the OECD inflation rates that, at long last, had just been damped down, the United States and other OECD governments adopted a no-nonsense, monetarist monetary policy that shot interest rates sky-high. This quickly confronted many newly industrializing and middle-income countries (which not only had borrowed heavily from foreign commercial banks during the 1970s, but also had accepted a large proportion of variable-interest-rate obligations) with increases in their debt-service bills that soon exceeded those in their oil bills.

[3] John W. Sewell, Peter M. Storm, and Contributors, *Challenges and Priorities in the 1990s: An Alternative U.S. International Affairs Budget, FY1993* (Washington, DC: ODC, 1992).

[4] United Nations Development Programme, *Human Development Report 1992* (New York: Oxford University Press, 1992), Ch. 3.

[5] Robert H. Cassen, *Does Aid Work?* (New York: Oxford University Press, 1986); The Task Force on Concessional Flows of the (joint) Development Committee of the World Bank and IMF, *Report and Aid for Development: The Key Issues*, 1985; Roger C. Riddell, *Foreign Aid Reconsidered* (Baltimore: Johns Hopkins Press, 1987); Commission on Security and Economic Assistance, Frank Carlucci, Chair, *Report to the Secretary of State*, 1983; Task Force on Development Organizations, Jimmy Carter, Chair, *The Carnegie Commission on Science, Technology, and Government, Report*, 1992.

[6] Stanley Please, *The Hobbled Giant: Essays on the World Bank* (Boulder: Westview, 1984), p. 27.

[7] World Bank, Country Economics Department, *Report on Adjustment Lending II* (1990).

[8] Barbara Ward, J. D. Runnalls, and Lenore D'Anjou, *The Widening Gap* (New York: Columbia University Press, 1971).

[9] Such lessons are discussed at greater length in John P. Lewis and contributors, *Strengthening the Poor: What Have We Learned?* U.S.-Third World Policy Perspectives No. 10 (New Brunswick, NJ: Transaction Publishers in cooperation with the ODC, 1988).

[10] Albert O. Hirschman, *Strategy of Economic Development* (New Haven, CT: Yale University Press, 1958).

[11] "Review of Structural Adjustment Lending" (R 81-64) April 1, 1981, p. 16.

[12] World Bank, Operations Evaluation Department, *Structured Adjustment Lending: A First Review of Experience*, Report No. 6409, Washington, DC, September 24, 1986, pp. 13–14.

[13] Organisation for Development Co-Operation, *Development Co-Operation 1987* (Paris: OECD, 1988), p. 75.

[14] Richard Jolly and Ralph van der Hoeven, "Editor's Introduction," and Richard Jolly, "Adjustment with a Human Face: A UNICEF Record and Perspective on the 1980s," in *World Development*, Vol. 19, No. 12, December 1991, pp. 1801–1821.

[15] Ibid. Also published for the first time in the same December 1991 issue of *World Development*, pp. 1823–34, a paper presented by UNICEF to the IMF in 1984, G.K. Helleiner, G.A. Cornia, and R. Jolly, "IMF Adjustment Policies and Approaches and the Needs of Children."

[16] Jolly, "Adjustment with a Human Face: A UNICEF Record and Perspective," op. cit., p. 1811.

[17] Frances Stewart, "The Many Faces of Adjustment," *World Development*, Vol. 19, No. 12, December 1991, pp. 1847–64; World Bank, Country Economics Department, "Third Report on Adjustment Lending," February 1992.

[18] World Bank, "Third Report on Adjustment Lending," op. cit.

[19] Ralph van der Hoeven, "Adjustment with a Human Face: Still Relevant or Overtaken by Events?" *World Development*, Vol. 19, No. 12, December 1992, p. 1841.

[20] See Jolly, "Poverty and Adjustment in the 1990s," in *Strengthening the Poor: What Have We Learned?* op. cit., Ch. 9.

[21] Organisation for Development Co-Operation, *Development Co-Operation 1986* (Paris: OECD, 1987), p. 107.

[22] UNICEF Executive Director and Deputy Director, respectively.

[23] Giovanni Andrea Cornia, Richard Jolly, and Frances Stewart (eds.), *Adjustment with a Human Face* (New York: Oxford University Press, Vol. I, 1987, Vol. II, 1988).

[24] "Structural Adjustment Lending . . . is nonproject lending to support programs of policy and institutional change necessary to modify the structure of an economy so that it can maintain both its growth rate and the viability of its balance of payments in the medium term." World Bank, *Operational Manual Statement No. 3.58*, Annex II, November 1982.

[25] World Bank, *Review of IDA Lending Allocation Criteria and Guidelines*, October 1989.

[26] World Bank, "Third Report on Adjustment Lending," op. cit.

[27] Such an expectation had been voiced by then-World Bank Vice President and Chief Economist Stanley Fischer in 1990.

[28] *A World of Difference: A New Framework for Development Cooperation in the 1990s* (The Hague: Ministry of Foreign Affairs, March 1991).

[29] World Bank, Resource Mobilization Department, *Review of National Aid Programs: Federal Republic of Germany*, August 1992.

[30] Ministry of Foreign Affairs, *Japan's ODA 1991*, Tokyo, March 1992.

About the Author

JOHN P. LEWIS is professor emeritus of economics and international affairs at the Woodrow Wilson School of Public and International Affairs of Princeton University. From 1979–1981 he served as chair of the Development Assistance Committee of the Organisation for Economic Co-operation and Development, and from 1969–1974 he was dean of the Woodrow Wilson School. From 1983–1992 he served as ODC's senior advisor and chair of the ODC's Program Advisory Committee; he continues today as senior advisor. His many publications include *Business Conditions Analysis, Quiet Crisis in India,* and *Development Co-Operation* (1979, 1980, and 1981). Currently, he is writing the authorized history of the World Bank with Richard Webb.

About the ODC

ODC fosters an understanding of how development relates to a much changed U.S. domestic and international policy agenda and helps shape the new course of global development cooperation.

ODC's programs focus on three main issues: the challenge of political and economic transitions and the reform of development assistance programs; the development dimensions of international global problems; and the implications of development for U.S. economic security.

In pursuing these themes, ODC functions as:

■ *A center for policy analysis.* Bridging the worlds of ideas and actions, ODC translates the best academic research and analysis on selected issues of policy importance into information and recommendations for policymakers in the public and private sectors.

■ *A forum for the exchange of ideas.* ODC's conferences, seminars, workshops, briefings bring together legislators, business executives, scholars, and representatives of international financial institutions and nongovernmental groups.

■ *A resource for public education.* Through its publications, meetings, testimony, lectures, and formal and informal networking, ODC makes timely, objective, nonpartisan information available to an audience that includes but reaches far beyond the Washington policymaking community.

ODC is a private, nonprofit organization funded by foundations, corporations, governments, and private individuals.

Stephen J. Friedman is the Chairman of the Overseas Development Council, and John W. Sewell is the Council's President.

Board of Directors

Overseas Development Council
SPECIAL PUBLICATIONS SUBSCRIPTION OFFER
Policy Essays • Policy Focus

As a subscriber to the ODC's 1993 publication series, you will have access to an invaluable source of independent analyses of U.S.-Third World issues—economic, political, and social—at a savings of at least 10% off the regular price.

Brief and easy-to-read, each **Policy Focus** briefing paper provides background information and analysis on a current topic on the policy agenda. In 1993, 6–8 papers will cover the Bretton Woods institutions and the former Soviet Union, the Global Environment Facility, the Generalized System of Preferences, and the implications of the North American Free Trade Area, among other topics.

Policy Essays explore critical issues on the U.S.-Third World agenda in 80-120 succinct pages, offering concrete recommendations for action. The two final essays in the "conditionality" series, *Pro-Poor Aid Conditionality* and *Global Goals, Contentious Means: Issues of Multiple Aid Conditionality*, will explore the potential utility of applying conditionality for the goal of poverty reduction and the implications of multiple aid conditionality—linking political, environmental, military, and pro-poor reforms to foreign aid.

Global Governance and Aid After the Earth Summit will assess the international institutional capabilities that now exist for carrying through on the UNCED commitments of sustainable development.

United States and Africa: Into the 21st Century examines the pressing regional challenges of ending civil conflict, expanding and consolidating democracy, and achieving economic recovery and sustainable growth. It also assesses options for future U.S. policy.

SUBSCRIPTION OPTIONS

Special Publications Subscription Offer* (all Policy Essays (5–6) and Policy Focus briefing papers (6–8) issued in 1993)	$65.00
1993 Policy Essay Subscription*	$50.00
Policy Focus Subscription*	$20.00

* Subscribers will receive all 1993 publications issued to date upon receipt of payment; other publications in subscription will be sent upon release. Book-rate postage is included in price.

All orders require prepayment. Visa and Mastercard orders accepted by phone or mail. Please send check or money order to:

O | D | C

Publication Orders
Overseas Development Council
1875 Connecticut Avenue, NW
Suite 1012
Washington, DC 20009
(202) 234-8701

ENVIRONMENT AND THE POOR: Development Strategies For A Common Agenda

H. Jeffrey Leonard and contributors

Few aspects of development are as complex and urgent as the need to reconcile antipoverty and pro-environmental goals. Do both of these important goals—poverty alleviation and environmental sustainability—come in the same package? Or are there necessary trade-offs and must painful choices be made?

A basic premise of this volume is that environmental degradation and intractable poverty are often especially pronounced in particular ecological and social settings across the developing world. These twin crises of development and the environment can and must be addressed jointly. But they require differentiated strategies for the kinds of physical environments in which poor people live. This study explores these concerns in relation to irrigated areas, arid zones, moist tropical forests, hillside areas, urban centers, and unique ecological settings.

The overview chapter highlights recent efforts to advance land and natural resource management, and some of the real and perceived conflicts between alleviating poverty and protecting the environment in the design and implementation of developing policy. The chapters that follow offer economic investment and natural resource management options for reducing poverty and maintaining ecological balance for six different areas of the developing world.

CONTENTS:

H. Jeffrey Leonard:	Overview
Montague Yudelman:	Sustainable and Equitable Development in Irrigated Environments
J. Dirck Stryker:	Technology, Human Pressure, and Ecology in the Arid and Semi-Arid Tropics
John O. Browder:	Developmental Alternatives for Tropical Rain Forests
A. John De Boer:	Sustainable Approaches to Hillside Agricultural Development
Tim Campbell:	Urban Development in the Third World: Environmental Dilemmas and the Urban Poor
Alison Jolly:	The Madagascar Challenge: Human Needs and Fragile Ecosystems

0 | D | C

U.S.-Third World Policy Perspectives, No. 11 1989, 256 pp.

ISBN: 0-88738-282-7 (cloth) $24.95

ISBN: 0-88738-786-1 (paper) $15.95

POVERTY, NATURAL RESOURCES, AND PUBLIC POLICY IN CENTRAL AMERICA

Sheldon Annis and contributors

Rural poverty and environmental degradation are steadily worsening in Central America, undercutting the prospects for regional peace and economic recovery. This volume analyzes strategies that aim to reduce poverty and protect the environment in the region. It lays out a policy agenda for both Central Americans and donor nations.

Poverty, Natural Resources, and Public Policy in Central America presents the latest thinking on five key challenges in the region. These include the equity and ecological consequences of traditional and nontraditional agricultural export strategies; procedures for non-governmental organizations and international agencies to promote sustainable development; the potential role of taxation for generating much-needed revenue and addressing the region's inequitable land distribution; the surge of cross-border environmental problems and their related political tensions; and finally the need to reconcile resource conservation with multiple human uses of tropical lands.

CONTENTS:

Sheldon Annis:	Overview
Oscar Arias and James D. Nations:	A Call for Central American Peace Parks
Stephen B. Cox:	Citizen Participation and the Reform of Development Assistance in Central America
Alvaro Umaña and Katrina Brandon:	Inventing Institutions for Conservation: Lessons from Costa Rica
Stuart K. Tucker:	Equity and the Environment in the Promotion of Nontraditional Agricultural Exports
John Strasma and Rafael Celis:	Land Taxation, the Poor, and Sustainable Development

Sheldon Annis is associate professor of geography and environmental studies at Boston University. He is the author of *God and Production in a Guatemalan Town* and co-editor of *Direct to the Poor: Grassroots Development in Latin America.*

O | D | C

U.S.-Third World Policy Perspectives, No. 17 Fall 1992, 280 pp.

ISBN: 1-56000-015-5 (cloth) $24.95

ISBN: 1-56000-577-7 (paper) $15.95

Policy Essay Series

Global Goals, Contentious Means:
Issues of Multiple Aid Conditionality

Joan M. Nelson

The final essay in ODC's aid conditionality series examines the implications of linking political, environmental, military, and pro-poor reforms to foreign aid. The author considers the varying levels of commitment of both donors and recipients to the goals, and the extent to which the goals are complementary or conflictive. She also assesses the circumstances under which conditionality is likely to be an effective means of achieving the desired objectives, and when other methods are more feasible and appropriate.

Policy Essay No. 10, Forthcoming Summer/Fall 1993
ISBN: 1-56517-012-1 $9.95

Global Governance and Aid After the Earth Summit

Maurice J. Williams and Patti L. Petesch

Following up on the 1992 U.N. Conference on Environment and Development requires greatly expanded development cooperation and new operational mechanisms. This essay assesses the international institutional capabilities that now exist for carrying through on the UNCED commitment of assistance for sustainable development and proposes policy changes for the future.

Policy Essay No. 9, Forthcoming Spring 1993
ISBN: 1-56517-011-3 $9.95

Pro-Poor Aid Conditionality

John P. Lewis

The road to poverty alleviation often requires governments of developing countries to alter their policies. In the last few years, donors have increasingly conditioned aid upon more vigorous reform efforts. This essay explores the extent to which the development community has and can in future apply conditionality for the goal of poverty reduction.

Policy Essay No. 8, May 1993
ISBN: 1-56517-009-1 $9.95

United States and Africa:
Into the Twenty-First Century

Carol J. Lancaster

The sweeping changes that have taken place in Africa, the tremendous challenges that remain, and a new U.S. administration make this a timely re-examination of U.S. policies toward the region. This essay reviews the major economic and political trends in the region since the era of independence. The pressing regional challenges of ending civil conflict, expanding and consolidating democracy, and achieving economic recovery and sustainable growth are examined, and issues and options for future U.S. policy toward Africa are assessed.

Policy Essay No. 7, April 1993
ISBN: 1-56517-010-5 $9.95

Pressing for Peace:
Can Aid Induce Reform?

Nicole Ball

With the end of the Cold War, aid donors and recipients are increasingly entering into discussions that include military expenditures in the context of overall government spending. Making economic aid contingent upon military reforms is one tool that can be used to promote change. The essay examines the different policy tools available to donors, with special emphasis on alternatives to conditionality and policy implications for the United States, developing countries, and the international community as a whole.

Policy Essay No. 6, 1992
ISBN: 1-56517-006-7 $9.95

North-South Environmental Strategies, Costs, and Bargains

Patti L. Petesch
Foreword by Maurice F. Strong

This study provides a road map of the principal measures that are proposed to slow climate change, deforestation, and species extinction, as well as the areas of agreement and disagreement between North and South. It assesses the potential costs to the developing world in stemming these global threats and discusses how these costs might complement or compete with other economic and environmental needs.

"a direct contribution to the UNCED process and the debate and action after the Earth Summit"

—The Centre for Our Common Future
July 1992

Policy Essay No. 5, 1992
ISBN: 1-56517-005-9 $9.95

Encouraging Democracy:
What Role for Conditioned Aid?

Joan M. Nelson with Stephanie J. Eglinton

There are calls for the use on conditioned aid as a powerful means to promote democracy in the developing countries. Not only bilateral aid programs, but the international financial institutions are also viewed as channels for pressing political reform. Is this a direct and powerful move toward tremendously important and appealing goals? Or, rather, a futile or even counterproductive path? The study takes a closer look at the logic of conditionality and the historical record and proposes future directions for its effective uses.

"Encouraging Democracy *is full of insightful and useful analysis*"

—Richard D. Erb
Deputy Managing Director
International Monetary Fund

Policy Essay No. 4, 1992
ISBN: 1-56517-004-0 $9.95

Debt Reductions and North-South Resource Transfers to the Year 2000

Richard E. Feinberg, Eduardo Fernández-Arias, and Frank Sader

Developing countries have had to pay considerably more in interest and amortization than they have been receiving in new loans from the international financial community. This essay presents the latest data on negative resource transfers and projections through the end of this century, including the potential impact of various debt reduction schemes on net flows.

Policy Essay No. 3, 1991
ISBN: 1-56517-002-4 $8.00

Debt Conversion in Latin America:
Panacea or Pandemic?

Mary L. Williamson

Chile's debt conversion program has had mixed results. While it has reduced debt, promoted foreign and domestic investment, accelerated economic restructuring, and assisted export growth, it has also subsidized foreign purchases of companies at already depressed prices, and investment has not necessarily been targeted toward desired sectors. This study explores Chile's experience and draws from it lessons for the Latin American debtors.

"a pleasure to read ... well-informed and balanced"

—Joaquín Vial
CIEPLAN, Chile

Policy Essay No. 2, 1991
ISBN: 1-56517-001-6 $8.00

Modular Multilateralism:
North-South Economic Relations in the 1990s

Richard E. Feinberg and Delia M. Boylan

Bipolarity's demise opens new opportunities for North-South cooperation, as previously unlikely alliances join to forge solutions of mutual benefit to common problems. ODC's study presents a decisionmaking model that focuses on multilateral institutions with memberships that vary according to issue and that cut across the old North-South divide. Case studies are based on current international problems.

"a creative approach, which is at once innovative and more practical"

—Joseph S. Nye
Center for International Affairs
Harvard University

Policy Essay No. 1, 1991
ISBN: 1-56517-000-8 $8.00

O | D | C

CHALLENGES AND PRIORITIES IN THE 1990S:

An Alternative U.S. International Affairs Budget FY1993

John W. Sewell, Peter M. Storm, and contributors

The massive political, social, and economic changes in the world over the last two years present an unprecedented opportunity to rethink an reorganize U.S. government budget priorities in the field of international affairs. The second in ODC's series of alternative international affairs budgets is offered to encourage debate over the policies needed to address key global challenges central to U.S. interests in the 1990s.

Special offer: Order *Challenges and Priorities in the 1990s* and receive at no additional cost the FY1992 alternative international affairs budget, *United States Budget for a New World Order.*

Reactions to *United States Budget for a New World Order:*

". . . I do commend you on the thought process and your spirit of innovation. It is precisely that which we need at this point in time."
— Frank Carlucci, former Secretary of Defense

"Many of your 'alternative budget' proposals would be worth pursuing."
— Lee H. Hamilton, U.S. House of Representatives

"Your ideas are certainly worthy of consideration by the Congress and the President as a starting point for debate."
— Charles S. Robb, U.S. Senate

ISBN: 1-56517-008-3 $9.95

O | D | C